FUELLED BY BELIEF

The Cityjet Story

Pat Byrne

The Liffey Press

Published by
The Liffey Press
Ashbrook House
10 Main Street
Raheny, Dublin 5, Ireland
www.theliffeypress.com

A catalogue record of this book is
available from the British Library.

ISBN 1-904148-57-3 (Paperback)
1-904148-63-8 (Hardback)

Printed in Spain by GraphyCems.

FUELLED BY BELIEF

CONTENTS

About the Author

Pat Byrne is a Dublin-based businessman who originally comes from Bray, County Wicklow, where he was educated at Presentation College.

Pat's business career is expansive. Probably better known for being the founder of Irish airline, Cityjet, which he ran as CEO for seven years, he had previously spent twenty years in the financial services sector. Having spent his very early years "serving his time" in the bank, he went on to develop Savings & Investments Limited, now known as Cornmarket, which became one of Ireland's most successful investment and insurance broking houses.

Nowadays Pat Byrne, in consort with his partners, acts as a business catalyst and mentor to business owners and managers, through their company, Rainmaker. He claims that the rainmaker style of engagement is more one of pragmatic interventionist than management consultant.

Pat is married to Jane and has two sons, Ross and Harry, and two daughters, Sarah and Eleanor from his previous marriage to Ann. This is his first book.

ACKNOWLEDGEMENTS

There are many people to mention because of their importance to this story, starting with the real players who were there with me at various stages in the heat of battle and whom I trust have equally fond and proud, if somewhat scary memories of what we did. So you guys please stand up and take a bow:

Kevin Barry, Luke Mooney, Miriam Matthews, Hugh Rodgers, Paddy O'Reilly, Pearse Gilroy, Sharon Ryan, Peter Ribeiro, Eileen Lawlor, Linda Corr, Nicola Watkins, Linda Kennedy, Ronan Murtagh, Laura Finnegan, Robbie Adams, Aidan Keane, Chris Curran, Tom Darcy, John O'Sullivan, John Power, Nicky Bridgett, Kemble Larkin, Cameron Smith, Simon Kay, Linda Mackesey, Orla McIntyre, Mick Meagher, Jimmy Martin, Jacques Bankir, Geoff White, Neil Hyde, Ray Mills, Ray Murray, Brian Tyrell, Noeleen McGrath, Tom Carney, Gwen Robinson, Denise Flynn, Ed Gohery, Viv Cullen, John Rogers, Ali Zadeh, Phil Fenton, John Barnwell, Maureen Melly, Ken Gough, Dave Shepard, Jocelyn Stephens, Patricia Nolan, Niamh Delmar, Maurice Power, Regina Smith, Damien Manly, Zarina Peer, Margaret Murphy, Jack Killock, Tommy Maxwell, Joe Smith, Emma Mangan, Lisa Byrne, Mike Ryan, Pat Bridgett, Margaret Hoare, Shelly Murphy, Trish Doherty, Mary Purcell, Katherine McGovern, Lisa Kilbride, Lisa McCabe, Natalie and Nicola O'Brien, Michael Collins, Paula Dunne, Joan Tighe, and to our hugely missed friend, Joyce Cox, who sadly passed on recently, and also not forgetting the late Captain Tony Doyle.

Many more people have been part of the Cityjet adventure and the full list would run to hundreds, so please forgive me for not mentioning every name. This in no way diminishes the value I put on the contribution made by every member of an extraordinarily committed bunch of people.

Without passengers, we would have had nothing and the enterprise would not have lasted a wet week. To those wonderful regular travellers who gave us their support and stayed with us, even though we tested their patience at times, I say a heartfelt "thank you" for your confidence in us. You gave us the platform from which we could build our business.

To a very responsive man who said "Yes, I will publish your story", when other publishing houses were saying "No thanks", David Givens of the Liffey Press has earned my profound gratitude and respect.

The really difficult thing about writing your first book is trying to answer the question, "Will anyone find this interesting enough to read it right through?" Well, I had some good friends who volunteered to read early iterations and give me their honest opinions. Thank you Sharon Tate, John Murphy, Barry Coleman, Luke Mooney, Noel Hiney, my parents, Paddy and Marie Byrne, my sister Anne and my wife, Jane. You lifted my confidence that this book might work.

Finally, to Jane who endured the living of this true experience (the writing of the book was the easy bit) through the good days and the not-so-good days: thanks for your constant encouragement and support all the way.

PREFACE

Striving is an interesting word. Winning or even losing are very clearly defined outcomes, but striving has no end. When you are striving you are operating on adrenalin fuelled by a cocktail made up of the prospect of succeeding countered in perfect balance by the fear of failure.

It doesn't matter if today you are crowned the champion. Tomorrow the fear of losing your top-of-the-heap status immediately propels your next steps. Equally, the experience of not reaching your goal in a particular endeavour often has the effect of enhancing your determination of going one better next time. It is all about *next time, another shot at it*, to prove either that *last time was no fluke* or *I'll show them this time what I really can do*.

Isn't it wonderful that we have this natural tendency not to accept anything as being over? As long as we hold onto that inner determination to get up and go again — quicker, harder, smarter, making use of whatever it is we think will give us an edge — we will get back in the game. And we will stay there until we get a result or at least for as long as we have the belief that we can survive against stiff competition and have a realistic prospect of being there or thereabouts.

Where does this drive come from? It is the willingness to participate unconditionally, the spirit to compete with no guarantee of a successful outcome.

In short, I believe this is the art of striving. It is a creed or code for life in all of its many aspects, be it sport, business, professional vocation, art, entertainment and above all else in your endeavour simply to be a successful person in whatever community you choose to be part of.

Win, lose or draw in any pursuit, it is about how we try and what we take from either victory or defeat. While it is a great feeling to know we gave it our best effort, its an even better feeling knowing that what we have learned from the experience gives us a better chance of success next time out. It is about refusing to embrace the concept of *never*. I live by it and it has served me well. This is what it has meant to me throughout a most extraordinary chapter of my business life.

Chapter One

THE WIND TUNNEL

From the time I was a small boy, I have always had ambition. The urge inside me to drive to achieve something is as familiar as the smell of sandwiches wrapped in bread paper and placed in my schoolbag, or the brand new leather smell of my first pair of rugby boots for my six-year-old feet.

My school days were mostly about rugby but I was also a relatively keen student, with English, and ultimately debating, being particular loves of mine. The latter was to prove itself very useful in years to come. My principal goal at secondary school was to be part of the winning team that would bring the Leinster Senior Cup home to Pres Bray after an absence of forty years. We got so very close — as far as the third minute of injury time of the Cup Final — before we let it slip from our grasp, losing to the 1971 star-spangled Belvedere side which would ultimately produce three senior internationals.

Throughout my schoolboy days, I also held onto an aspiration to be a pilot, going as far as undergoing the flight crew selection process with the RAF at Biggin Hill in 1970, while in my final year at school. I was offered an officer's commission by the RAF, not as a fast jet pilot but rather to be trained as an air traffic controller. If you've ever been a Biggles fan like I was, then you'll know there wasn't a single page devoted to the exploits of the heroic air traffic controller. So the RAF lost a good man and Chase Bank gained a winner. Or so I tried to tell them.

Joining the bank at seventeen, with a good pensionable job for the next forty years or more, didn't quite fire my imagination but the prospect of being sent to Trinity College while remaining on the payroll certainly did appeal. To be fair to the bank, it was never a guarantee but on being hired I was told the prospects of me swapping bank clerking for toughing it out on campus were reasonably good. Sadly, by the time the new academic term came around, the leaves fell and so too did my remote prospects of donning the famed colours of Trinity. There was a change in policy in the bank which decreed no more free rides through college.

The new order called for accountancy and the best deal on offer was blocks of study leave and payment of night class fees for aspiring employees with ambition. I chose marketing by night without bank support. The attack on marketing through academia soon gave way to the practice of selling cable television by evening to earn as much again as my meagre salary from Chase. I was struggling to run my Volkswagen Beetle and go steady, all on £72 a month. Receiving customers of the bank and responding to their needs over the counter by day was the complete inverse of my nocturnal experience in pushing cable TV door-to-door.

But breaks came; they always have for me. How much I have contributed to the strokes of good fortune that come my way and how much is down to good luck is an unresolved question. I have always believed, however, that all of us can play a major part in making our own good luck through positive actions. Similarly, we are often the authors of some of our bad luck through inaction or carelessness. Positioning and timing are very valuable assets.

Anyway, it happened during a humdrum point in my day when I was handing over the customised denominations of bank notes and coin to a large corporate customer for dispensing as the weekly payroll. There he was, next in line. He was familiar, because he called to the bank counter, and to me particularly, on a frequent basis. I knew his company, Savings & Investments, was some sort of insurance/investment brokerage. We had built up a reasonable rapport. He was always well turned-out, professional-looking, with a deep voice that commanded respect. "I can see you really are enjoying yourself in this job," he delivered in the laconic tones of a Walter Matthau.

I was taken aback somewhat by the straight observation, and it was clear I was letting my slip show more than a bit. I had been caught in a bad mood and obviously the vibes I was transmitting were pretty raw. That didn't stop me making a sarcastic response. "Yeah, I suppose you'll give me a £1,300-a-year job and a company car!" When I heard the sound of my own voice being outrageously blunt to this familiar yet unknown quantity, I began to get a grip. This could go horribly wrong, I thought. "No," he said. "I won't give you £1,300 a year but you could start on £1,100 and prove that you're worth more." By this stage, I thought, to hell with caution; there was no going back on this one. "And the car?" I asked. "Oh yes, you'll need that," he said. "Well, what do we do next?" I queried, trying not to bottle it. "Come to our office in Dawson Street for an interview with one of my colleagues on Tuesday after work and we'll see where we might go."

That was it. He was Mervyn Percival. Although neither of us knew it at the time, one of the most successful partnerships in the Life and Investment broking business in Ireland had just been born. The fact that I was just twenty years of age and he thirteen years my senior would certainly not have suggested that such a dynamic pairing was about to emerge. I entered Savings & Investments, or S&I as we liked to call ourselves, in January 1974, when the company was less than two years old.

S&I solicited for new clients through the placement of prominent advertisements on the front pages of the *Irish Times* and *Irish Independent* newspapers. People clipped the coupon and sent us their contact details together with their preferred level of regular monthly investment. Our job was to make contact with these "prospects" and make an appointment to see them to persuade them to proceed with the investment. This was so different from working in the bank. For a start, there was no set day, as the morning could begin in the office or on a visit to a prospect. There certainly was no early end to the day as it was expected of us to use evening time to visit people who could not see us during their working day.

However, by the onset of autumn, just eight months after I joined S&I, the company was in crisis. The recession in Britain had finally taken hold of the Irish economy also. We saw it quite graphically through the complete drying-up of coupons flowing in the door from our expensive ad campaigns. The pressure came on quickly when one of the three principals — the one who had interviewed me the previous December and sold me an Irish Life investment plan — was the first to go "to pursue other interests". Then it got closer: two of the three directors, to whom we new recruits were apprenticed, were forced out on the basis of poor sales performance.

One by one, my colleagues and I were called in for the dreaded review of our sales figures. I was on target, although I was finding it a nightmare to dig up business, with no leads being supplied by the company after the failure of the ad campaign. Some opted to leave. Suddenly the small brokerage, which had been on an aggressive expansion path, was quite small again, with no obvious marketing strategy to win business from an increasingly nervous market who feared for their livelihoods with every new announcement of company closures and rising inflation. Things were getting rough.

It was late afternoon on a Friday in November 1974 and I was sitting in the living room of an existing client of S&I who had bought an investment plan almost two years previously. I was on a re-canvass mission, trying to see if I could sell a top-up plan to this client. Going though the fact-find about his finances, it became obvious that the man could not even afford to take out another £10 per month plan. Then something caught his eye. It was the blue flower sticking out of the neck of a bottle in my briefcase.

The bottle and flower were actually illustrations on a leaflet from Friends Provident; the product involved was permanent health insurance. "What's that?" my man asked. "That's not for you; you don't need it. You're already covered for that type of thing. After all, you're a teacher and the state provides well for you."

"You're wrong," he told me. "Listen to me. I'm the secretary to our local branch of the Irish National Teachers Organisation and we've been collecting ten pence a week from our members over the past twenty years to help support a young teacher who became incapacitated through a football accident."

The genie (not the flower) was now well and truly out of the bottle. Here was a glaring gap in the employment conditions of those considered most protected. Teachers, who exhausted more than fifty-two weeks in sick leave in any consecutive four-year period, were put out on disability pension which only amounted to whatever their service length to date would give them in pension benefits.

We found an underwriter in the UK who was prepared to relax the entry conditions for teachers joining what was going to be a voluntary scheme. This was a big risk for the underwriter because he could be stuck with all the bad risks and not enough of the healthy trout. Success for everybody was going to come down to sheer hard selling in every school in Ireland. Staff rooms and national teachers' branch meetings in hotel ballrooms were going to be our stamping ground for the foreseeable future as we went on our enrolment blitz. It was hard going, made all the more difficult by some factions within the union who disagreed with the decision of the INTO's National Executive Committee to facilitate the promotion of this non-compulsory scheme. We got lucky, as the Association of Secondary Teachers in Ireland approached us for a similar scheme. We had to find a second underwriter for the secondary teachers' scheme because the one we had for the INTO scheme was struggling with a disappointing take-up level of members to that point and would have no appetite for another adventure, until the first one had proved itself viable. We redirected our energies into promoting the new scheme. It was a phenomenal success, so much so that the INTO asked to renew our efforts with the promise that the internal resistance to what we were trying to do would be contained effectively. It was, and we achieved the targets. A collective sigh of relief from our worried underwriters, from the unions who had run the risk of getting egg on their faces, and of course from us.

If we could sell teachers one financial product, then we could sell them others. We needed new innovative offers and the means of handling huge volume processing. I set up our own technology subsidiary and we got to grips quickly with the potential modern systems needed for accelerating our growth. Arguably, we were the leaders in technological development involving deduction of premiums at payroll source and interfacing with multiple insurers. We designed more offers and so successful was our ability to sell through our nationwide sales force that we were enjoying a cross-product holding of 2.5 products per teacher on our books. Nurses were our next target market; we repeated the formula with a moderate success rate, but nonetheless this market sector also remained extremely financially viable.

Throughout this heady growth phase, I had been made a director of the company at 22, and Managing Director by the tender age of 27, when I had advanced my equity holding in the company to 40 per cent. We now had 50,000 clients and a staff of 125. We were making good profits. I began to look over my shoulder. I was worried about protecting what we had built up and I was searching for a way for us to capitalise on what we had achieved by way of taking some of our winning chips off the table. We had created value in the company and I felt it would be prudent to realise some of this by way of a partial sale of equity to a bigger player.

I went on a "get us noticed" campaign with some well-positioned articles in the media about our progress and our unique ability in the area of affinity marketing. Sean Fitzpatrick of Anglo

Irish Bank came calling and we talked and speculated about the potential fit which Savings & Investments might represent for his growing bank. But within a few weeks, suddenly — and literally — in the door burst Craig McKinney of Woodchester Investments plc. Allied Irish Investment Managers had prompted him to take a look at us, and he didn't waste any time. With his highly capable Lieutenant of the time, David Dilger, the deal was negotiated over the following six weeks. It was worth a lot of money to us, as they wanted seventy-five per cent of our equity. There was an earn-out year with the lion's share of the purchase price riding on our performance against a stiff profit target. KPMG were very thorough in their audit, but the figures we delivered were for real. Woodchester had to pay the full shilling to us.

Over the previous years, Mervyn, as Chairman, and I, as Managing Director, had had a good partnership style of working. I was the "hands-on" guy and Mervyn adopted a more reflective style; I ran the company while we collaborated on strategic growth and managing the relationships with our trade union clients and the insurance companies. It worked really well. We complemented each other with our different approaches and skill sets. We also had a deep friendship. When we became part of Woodchester, the dynamic between us altered quite quickly. Mervyn became attracted to the higher profile of a PLC and Craig McKinney cultivated a relationship with him. I had ambition to go on growing the business within the Woodchester Group, especially as there was another earn-out on the remaining twenty-five per cent in five years' time. McKinney wanted me to become Group Marketing Director for his rapidly expanding operations, which were now spreading into the UK and Portugal. We didn't agree. Mervyn wanted to be more involved in the day to running of operations, a role which he had happily left to me for years. I felt he was muscling in after all the hard work and the tension developed between us and escalated rapidly. Both of us were at fault: two big egos and not enough space; something was going to give.

I could have taken the easy route and accommodated him but in truth I was beginning to realise that the passion I had always had for moving forward was dissipating. Woodchester were not overly supportive in funding my acquisition strategy of bolting on other brokerages to our business, as they felt leasing held the key to their growth. There were seriously difficult things going in my life at that time and my normally reliable intuitive judgement was most probably adversely affected. I went into a boardroom battle which, any other time, I would have known I simply couldn't win. Just as I had learned in rugby many years earlier, you don't take to the pitch carrying an injury because impaired performance doesn't rate. Stay fit and well or stay at home, especially it you want to play with the big boys!

Falling on my sword was painful. The company I had enormously contributed to building and which I had the privilege of leading was suddenly no longer at the centre of my commercial life. I had stamped my personality on the company. I had picked most of the management team and was committed to the personal and professional development of the staff. I had championed the technology play that gave us the platform for high volume growth and I personally designed most of the innovative financial services we had successfully delivered to our customer base.

I had developed an incisive understanding into relationship selling and marketing. The amount of one-on-one selling and group presentations I had performed over those seventeen years was incredible. My closure rate in sales conversions was huge and my attrition rate in lapsed clients was minimal. To me, a sales scenario was like two people sitting down to dinner together. When they get up from the table, they both feel they could have eaten more but are glad they didn't. It's about knowing there is a tomorrow and a day after that and you always want to be confident you can do more business together again.

I had a profound sense about what it takes to build a successful business. I knew it started and ended with establishing the relevance of what you have to offer to the lives of your customers, creating a dependency in them on what you can provide and committing to delivering a quality service before, during and after the sale, every time. Of course, there's a whole heap of support machinery, process and practice that sits behind all of this but if the outcome doesn't fly with your customer, the whole effort is wasted.

It was 1991. I was thirty-seven years old and still a young man of substantial means with a lot of unfilled potential and a whole lot to go on proving to myself. It was too early for retirement.

Chapter Two

I WANT TO BUILD AN AIRLINE

I was always interested in flying. As a small boy in my back garden in Bray, I would look up to confirm what my ears knew to to be another Vickers Viscount with the beautifully balanced pitch of its four engines unmistakably different from the smaller Fokker Friendship and its higher-pitched twin Rolls Royce darts. The east coastline was the favoured routing for air traffic to and from the UK in those days, with the crossing being made off Wexford.

I had taken it further and learned to fly, and quite a while before I actually found myself in the airline business I was the owner of a seriously good small aircraft. In fact, I had made that same journey in my plane over my childhood back garden to make the crossing to the UK many times. Sometimes business, more times pleasure. Always interesting.

I didn't wake up one morning and say, *I'm going to set up an airline*. I began dabbling in aircraft as a business shortly after I had exited the financial services world, leasing military training aircraft to the Irish Air Corps. Not my best business venture. It was supposed to be a sure thing, the short-term lease of three aircraft over one summer that was going to convert into a purchase. There was precedent. Take the risk. They need the planes. Big upside. So a hangar in Denton, Texas and my bank account both gave up some treasure. The three little aerial Ferraris were ferried across the Atlantic to Baldonnel airbase outside Dublin. *Of course* you won't be stuck with them!

Not everybody gets to own three new SIAI Marchetti SF 260 fully aerobatic machines. I did. But looking at the bright side, I learned how to fly a high-performance aircraft properly, thanks to the expert tuition of my Air Corps friends, Paul Deevy, John Mulvaney and Martin Duffy. I also met Kevin Barry, who would turn out to be a pivotal player in the next chapter of my business life.

I can't remember where they got my name from, but British Aerospace came to see me in April 1992. They were having a tough time convincing Aer Lingus about the merits of the BAe 146 regional jet. They felt a local perspective and flavour might add something to the sales effort. So I swatted up on the technical blurb and with my good friend and mentor Luke Mooney, we went off to see the fleet planning guru in the national airline. The meeting didn't last the hour. He postured as though he was the source of all aviation knowledge. The aircraft was rubbished. The notion of using this specialist short field performance jet airliner to launch a new route to London City Airport seemed to highly amuse our host. The arrogance was hard to take. Ten minutes later, we parked ourselves in front of two coffees in Kealy's pub in Cloghran. That's where and when the germination started.

I recounted to Luke my flirtation with London City Airport some three years earlier, shortly after it had been built. Having sold a majority stake in S&I to Woodchester, I had been enthusiastically reading myself into the part of the committed young PLC executive now playing in a bigger game. Woodchester had just opened a UK base in London's Canary Wharf and I began to explore the possibility of a quasi-private business shuttle between Dublin and London City Airport. I had taken things reasonably far, in as much as I negotiated with Dornier who manufactured a nineteen-seat turboprop called the 228 capable of operating into what was then an even shorter airfield. I approached Ryanair's CEO of the time, P.J. McGoldrick with a view to placing the 228 on their licence. Woodchester would pick up the tab for the lease, the crew and all operating costs, with a margin in it for the airline. P.J., with all of his experience rejected the idea on the sound commercial grounds that to operate one return service a day wouldn't justify the cost of a crew dedicated to this one aircraft type.

Of course, P.J. was right, but things had moved on since. The runway could now take a jet — the BAe 146 — and millions had been spent on building a direct roadway, including a major tunnel section from Docklands into the City.

As we embraced our mugs of coffee in Kealy's, against a background of late-morning pinters, our blissful naivety resolved the pair of us to forget about acting as agents for British Aerospace trying to sell planes. We were after the gap Aer Lingus had declared they were leaving open: a new route from Dublin to London City Airport. We knew it was going to take an enormous amount of detailed research into a business of which we understood the square root of damn-all. We also knew it would take a massive amount of planning, the harnessing of operational expertise, an incredible marketing plan and a ton of money. But the possibility of a true business service alternative for people who were fed up with Aer Lingus, Heathrow and tubes had to also spell big opportunity. But setting up a new business air corridor also meant establishing an airline. So . . . ?

Luke and I called on British Aerospace in Hatfield pretty quickly to determine just how badly these guys wanted to see their aircraft operate in Irish airspace. They were really stuck with a load of BAe 146s, which had been grounded by US-based airline customers who had dramatically fallen foul of the dreaded "scope agreements" with pilot unions. These scope agreements defined salary levels consistent with the number of seats on the aircraft type they were flying. After protracted deliberation, the magic number of seventy seats had emerged, above which fuller pilot salaries had to be paid. Game, set and match against the BAe 146 in America. At anything from eighty-five to ninety-four seats, depending on configuration, the BAe 146 series 200, the most prolifically produced model of the type on the US market, was not flavour of the month. Too many seats taking it past the seventy-seat "scope" threshold and not enough seats to make it worthwhile paying big salaries. The Nevada desert began to play landlord to whole rows of 146s as they were retired very prematurely from service by carriers.

The depth of the BAe problem ran to about a stg£700 million hole in the balance sheet unless they could get about 100 aircraft back in the air with revenue flowing in from leases. And here we were, setting ourselves up to be their first victims.

No, of course they didn't think we were mad talking about setting up an airline with absolutely no knowledge of what it takes and how to do it. Why would they? They saw a couple of guys who would get their new asset management company off the ground with an initial piece of business. Everybody knows critical mass has its origins in an original trickle and they had been on all of the courses. This was the beginning of a rollercoaster commercial relationship, not exactly the sort prescribed in the Harvard Book of Business. For better or worse, the about-to-be-born little airline was going to be tied to British Aerospace for a long time.

Aircraft selection was both the making and breaking of the business proposition for the airline. Choosing to operate into London City Airport determined the BAe 146 as the only choice of jet that could fly in there. Commencing a new route between Dublin and London was adding capacity on Europe's biggest route. However, flying to London City Airport would give us a decided point of differentiation in tempting regular business passengers away from Heathrow, Gatwick and Stansted.

London City Airport (LCY) was unique in many respects. It was close to downtown, just eight miles from the Stock Exchange. The time it took from wheels touching on the runway to a passenger disembarking, walking a short few steps to the compact terminal to getting into a taxi took less than five minutes. The trip into town would take on average twenty-five minutes. Compared to other airports, and Heathrow in particular, the time from

wheels on to getting into a taxi or the tube was twenty minutes
with lots of walking. The trip into town, via Heathrow Express to
Paddington took fifty-five minutes. The passenger experience at
LCY was pleasant. It was a throwback to the grand old days of
flying, with leather seats in the lounge, no overcrowding and no
long walks. You could see your aircraft outside the window, just
yards away.

The Cityjet business proposition was simple. We wanted to
combine the convenience and comfort of LCY with a proper on-
board business service that would be the talk of the business
community. Real customer care being delivered by enthusiastic
competent staff with a real positive attitude towards passengers.
We wanted to identify with the business passenger in a way
which said *we know what upsets and irritates you about regular travel
and we know we can make it better for you*. No airline junk food but
tasty meals and good wine, served from the bottle by the hostess.

We were determined to distinguish ourselves from the "low-
fares" airlines, as exemplified by Ryanair. The Ryanair model is
based on volume sales at a comparatively lower average fare.
Costs are controlled ruthlessly, which is why they avoid flying to
the more established and expensive airports. To get volume, they
use price as a magnet. The internet is their distribution medium
nowadays, and they suffer no dilution from agents' commission
or credit card charges. They push their workforce to produce
more flights per aircraft per day. Typically, Ryanair will get
twenty to twenty-five per cent more flying per day out of their
aircraft than their competitors. The turnaround times for aircraft
are rapid, assisted by operating into less congested airports, having no on-board catering to load and off-load and not cleaning the
cabin between flights. No seat allocation and the minimum of systems for check-in all help to keep costs down.

Therefore the Ryanair model is predicated on more flights per
aircraft per day, with more passengers per flight each producing a
moderate profit which, when aggregated over the enormous

number of flights operated by the airline, produces a huge bottom-line result. The compelling reason for people to choose to fly Ryanair was price. Passengers traded their expectations of customer care and the right to complain in exchange for the lowest possible fare. It didn't matter much if the airport Ryanair flew to was miles away from the city of destination; at least it was in the same country. Ryanair's passengers were predominantly people who were time rich and financially poor — at least in terms of what they were prepared to allocate towards their travel budgets.

Ryanair operated the indestructible Boeing 737 200 series which rarely went unserviceable and could take a lot of punishment. This aircraft selection, plus pilots who were prepared to be pushed extremely hard, essentially was the secret to their being able to operate so many flights per aircraft per day. The airline also felt completely unencumbered from having to provide a user-friendly service, nor did they live in fear of passenger backlash because they never operated a customer complaints department. It was, and still is, a "take it or leave it" proposition. They attained critical mass quickly and this helped them continue to defy gravity. The more people they flew, the more confident they grew in managing their suppliers, to the point of dominant arrogance. The best of luck to them, as it has been a phenomenal commercial success story. However, I personally don't subscribe to the culture in Ryanair promoted by Michael O'Leary.

Cityjet was a different model entirely. We targeted the business market where the audience was time poor and hopefully a little more financially well off. In the vast majority of cases, our business travellers had their fares paid for by their companies. It mattered a whole lot to these passengers to be delivered to an airport adjacent to where they were going to work. Our target market also were used to being looked after reasonably well on flights by Aer Lingus. Matching this standard of service wasn't enough; we to had significantly surpass it. This type of service cost a lot of money to provide and so we had to recover this in our fares. With

LCY we had an airport that was specialised, very expensive to operate into in terms of their charges and which had restrictions on its operating hours, such as lights out at 9.00 pm, practically no flying on Saturdays and only opening from noon on Sundays.

Getting back to the technical planning, there was a problem: the BAe 146 had four engines. Four engines are normally twice as expensive to run as two engines. Fairly simple sums, you might think. However, the 146 was in a league of its own as its particular engine, the ALF 502 was a one-off. Originally manufactured by Textron Lycoming, the 502 started out in life as a battle-tank gas turbine engine. When the Brits came up with their design for a regional jet airliner with exceptional short airfield performance, they required a wing that would give outstanding lift capability. Textron Lycoming came up with the wing design and they also could supply four little engines instead of two bigger ones, which would have diminished the aerodynamic properties of the super-lift wing.

Most jet engines on airliners manufactured in the 1980s, as was the case for the 146, have an average on-wing time before scheduled removal for overhaul of anything from 7,000 cycles to 9,000 cycles. The engine manufacturer of the ALF 502 published a TBO (time before overhaul) of 5,000 cycles. In each of our first three years of operation, we averaged less than 3,000 cycles per engine. So in going back to the theory that four engines are twice as expensive as two, I would suggest in the case of the 146 and its infamous 502 engine, the reality was that four were three times more expensive than two. It didn't take us long to figure out what BAe stood for — "Bring another engine".

In as much as we were embarking on an interesting journey with British Aerospace, so too would we have a testing time with the engine manufacturer. In the seven years I was to be CEO of the airline, the engine manufacturer went through a number of parentage changes. Textron Lycoming was bought by Allied Signals, who were subsequently taken out by Honeywell. At each changing of the guard, new promises were made that support for this engine would improve dramatically. New owners meant new people with whom we had to build new relationships. Trying to work with a short maintenance-interval engine is difficult for an emerging airline. Having to cope with numerous changes in the organisation supporting the product made it even more challenging. But the engineering support from the manufacturer did get better and promises began to be kept.

We also developed a keen preventative maintenance bias in our approach which paid handsome dividends as our affair with this unique powerplant deepened. We carried out non-mandatory inspections such as daily oil samples from the engines. We would send these off to the lab for analysis to tell us, for example, if the engine was "making metal" — shedding tiny fragments through friction. This might influence us to take an engine off the wing ahead of its scheduled removal date rather than risk a failure during operations. Oil, just like blood, can give valuable early warning of impending problems.

Valuable contacts were obtained from BAe in terms of who might help us evaluate route economics. We were given an introduction to Moritz Suter, CEO of Crossair, at the time Europe's leading regional airline. Moritz was extremely helpful, which he put down to his affection for the Irish. He actually loaned us his senior adviser for a few days to help us shape our initial thinking on how we might frame our business plan.

Meanwhile, it was critical to obtain a licence from the Irish authorities. This was late 1992 and the Department of Transport was still the power in all things aviation. The Irish Aviation Authority (IAA) was yet to be established, although a halfway house in the form of a State agency called ANSO had been established as an interim step to full devolution to a standalone regulatory body. As it happened, Luke was a good acquaintance of the Assistant Secretary of the Department of Transport, Michael McDonald. One afternoon in late autumn, we walked into his office to find out what would be required of us in the matter of applying for a licence to operate a scheduled airline service out of Dublin. We left two hours later, a lot wiser, if somewhat daunted by the enormity of the task ahead.

It was very clear that I needed to hire some outside help with a particular aptitude for writing airline licence applications or, to give it its correct title, an Aircraft Operators Certificate (AOC). But then there was Kevin Barry. Having resigned his commission with the Air Corps and bringing to a close his distinguished service as a superb military pilot, Kevin's promise of a job with Transaer didn't materialise. Transaer's loss was Business City Direct's enormous gain. (Yes, that's what we originally planned on calling the airline and in fact was the original name of the company we constituted in September 1992. A bit of a mouthful, certainly; it took me another four months to come up with the name Cityjet.)

Kevin is a consummate professional. He was determined to ensure that our application for an AOC was absolutely consistent with the emerging guidelines of the new EU joint aviation authorities' (JAA) template. In fact, by the time we eventually were awarded our licence, it was the very first new-style JAA-compliant certificate granted in Europe.

The slog for that licence was huge. It meant writing several manuals from scratch, covering all aspects of the proposed business ranging from flight operations to training, maintenance, etc. Kevin concentrated on all of the aerocrat aspects of the application while I set about solving the not insignificant issue of funding. The accepted rule of thumb at the time was that any new airline would be required to demonstrate a capital adequacy equivalent to three months' operating budget as per its own business plan and assuming zero revenue over the same period. I also focused on developing the marketing strategy, which was going to be crucial for our survival on the most competitive route between two cities in Europe.

I leaned heavily on Luke for support from his knowledge of private investors. To get this thing moving, we needed some seed capital before we could talk seriously to institutional investors. In the meantime I was personally funding the fledgling company. In addition to Kevin, we were joined by Pearse Gilroy, an accountant and friend who had performed brilliantly as an external service provider to Savings & Investments during the heady days of development throughout the mid-1980s. There was a mounting burden of administration and physical construction of manuals and documentation which was handled by Jane Corcoran, my partner at the time and now happily my wife. It wasn't long before we needed some maintenance expertise and a good working knowledge of how the engineering section of the Department of Transport worked and more importantly what they looked for. Paddy O'Reilly joined the team initially as a consultant and ultimately to become our Chief Engineer and Technical Director. And so the cottage industry trundled along.

I was burning cash. Apart from wages, office rent and materials, there were a lot of trips back and forth to British Aerospace, London City Airport management and also to Switzerland where Crossair continued to give us moral support and sound advice. I also had my Air Corps hangover in the form of the three Marchetti aircraft with their maintenance, insurance and bank interest hanging around my neck while struggling to re-market them, even at a very much reduced price to what I had paid for them.

We finally secured some seed capital from Frank Woods, an investor who had a keen personal interest in aviation and who liked what we were attempting to do. This took considerable pressure off me as the cash outflow burden was now being shared. It also gave me a crucial vote of confidence at a time when I was beginning to think there had to be an easier way of building a business. By spring of 1993, British Aerospace were getting impatient. Why were we not signing for aircraft deliveries? In parallel with this, I had been negotiating with London City Airport for slots and reduced landing and handling charges. Cityjet was a virtual airline long on ambition and very short on cash — no planes and still yet to be granted a licence. But we kept people on side and I believe they were absolutely impressed with our commitment to getting there. By June 1993 we decided on a big move. We packed up our bits and pieces and removed ourselves on a Friday night from Orchard House in Clonskeagh on Dublin's southside to take up residence in the terminal building at Dublin Airport.

This was probably the closest we had come to touching an aircraft. We could see plenty of them outside the office window, but none of them was ours. We were still not a licensed airline and we had no meaningful capital, yet. But we were striving with purpose. I was in promising talks with three institutions with whom I had done financial services business in my broker years. Luke was playing a blinder in getting us in front of more private investors. A classic scenario was developing. The institutions would like to see a good chunk of private money going in first and of course the private investors wanted the comfort of knowing the institutions would get involved. We pressed ahead with our aircraft lease negotiation with BAe and we agreed terms with London City Airport.

The strain was getting heavier. We were close to signing investors but they were not on board yet. The schedule of meetings with potential equity participants was exhausting. The presentations were always very in-depth, as they had to be when you are asking people to take a chance on putting money into a high-risk business being launched by a management team with no previous airline experience. I got in front of most of Ireland's wealthiest to make my pitch. I was hopeful of convincing Dr Tony O'Reilly in particular, because I felt not only that he had the capacity for serious funding but also that his background presence would lend weight to our efforts to get the best possible terms out of suppliers. The good doctor had a specific reason to be interested, as his daughter, Susan, was completing her commercial pilot training at Oxford Air Training College. Maybe it was my dogged persistence or his reluctance to say "no" to a trier, but the firm "maybe" that seemed to be the message coming from his camp only served to prolong yet another of the many hot trails I pursued over the hectic months of 1993. It would and it did eventually grow cold.

There were other tremendously supportive potential individual investors like Brendan McDonald, Mike Murphy and Seamus Gallagher. In fairness to these men, none of whom had said "no", all were understandably reluctant to be the first to commit. Thankfully, all of these people did eventually become shareholders in Cityjet. Sadly, Seamus died tragically later that year and his wife Veronica pressed ahead with the investment she knew he had wanted to make.

Meanwhile the absence of cash was life-threatening to the aspiring enterprise. We very soon would need to put deposits down on aircraft or they would not be delivered on time. To have credibility with potential investors, we had to demonstrate that we would definitely get our licence. To secure an approval in principle, we had to demonstrate to the Department of Transport that we had the capital adequacy, which on our projected level of activity amounted to IR£3.0 million (€3.81 million). We were at the centre of a rapidly spinning circle of evolving scenarios that all had an unhealthy "Catch 22" interdependency on each other.

To make our self-imposed launch date of the following January, we would have to start taking on one or two suitably qualified senior captains to help develop the training and crew selection infrastructure. We had already decided on contracting out our line maintenance function to an approved UK organisation, Hunting Aircraft and they, understandably, were looking for a cash commitment to start putting things in place to locate their team of engineers in Dublin. We had to find a way of making someone blink first to break this circular bind. I was decidedly uneasy.

Luke got us in front of an entrepreneur of legendary standing in Ireland. We met a number of times before we got to an understanding. The upshot of what we eventually agreed was that this man would underwrite our capital adequacy, in the sense that he would make available a deposit account containing IR£3.0 million which could be used to demonstrate to the authorities that we had the money. This would trigger the issuing of a letter of intent to grant the licence.

In equity terms, this special form of support from our benefactor cost us. But we needed to maintain forward momentum and this was the price of it. Having this confirmed intent to license was critical if we were to stay the pace and maintain credibility with the various parties with whom we were in negotiation around the future provision of vital services to the new airline. We were now no longer a few guys talking about setting up an airline; we had passed the test of competence with the licensing authority.

The one substantial detail, however, relating to this "underwriting" of our capital adequacy was that under no circumstances were we allowed, by he who owned the cash, to spend one penny of it. In short, we still had to find IR£3.0 million of real investor money that we could use. So the roadshows went on with the same cat-and-mouse activity of inching the private investors and the institutions towards making a commitment. Who would jump first?

I also had a huge issue about sales and marketing. My dilemma was simple. I had confidence that we could solicit support from the Dublin-based business community who would want to try our whole new alternative way of commuting to and from London. Our marketing was going to be provocative in its challenge to customers about the way they waste time in flying *near* London instead of *to* London. We would concentrate on the agoraphobia of congested airports and length of walks to and from planes. Above all else, we would promise to put the zest back into flying by making it an enormously enjoyable and comfortable service delivered by enthusiastic people who really put customer care first and meant it, especially on the bad days. The regular battle-hardened business frequent traveller would test our assertion of the comparative time-saving and when they tried our new style service we had to be sure we would be quids-in on retention of their custom. That was fine for Dublin, being the village that it is.

London was a whole other issue. We would be selling flights to Dublin out of an airport that the City had rejected through bad press and non-supporting corporate travel agents. The burning issue was transport access and the fact that the airport was located near where people worked in the City but not near where they lived. The tradition for British-based business people had always been to fly from an airport near their home, not their office. All of these challenges were surmountable, but over time. We would not have that time on funding of only IR£3.0 million. It was great to think about filling planes on our two early flights out of Dublin in the morning, comfortable in the knowledge that the same bums would occupy the seats on the way back of City on our evening flights. But where the business would sink or swim was going to be on our degree of success at winning London-originating traffic, and quickly. We desperately needed a killer formula.

Chapter Three

I'D LIKE TO RENT YOUR BRAND, RICHARD!

It was summer 1993. As has happened many times in my preoccupation with building a business, an idea wafted my way as if by some force of nature. The one person in business whom I really admired above all others at that time in my life was Richard Branson. I had never met him. I was a watcher from a distance and what I saw impressed me hugely. He had taken brave steps, challenged the establishment and endeared himself to the people as their special type of public schoolboy-sounding Robin Hood. To my mind, he was iconic.

Not for the first time did I look to Luke Mooney. This time I needed a telephone number of someone who could give me Branson's. Within an hour I was talking to a woman whom I thought was Branson's PA. (I would soon find out that he operated a team of three excellent PAs.) I wanted to talk to Richard if I could, I explained. "What's it about?" she asked.

"I'm starting this airline for business people to fly them from Dublin to London City Airport and I think Richard should meet with me as I believe he will find there is an exciting opportunity for Virgin to work with us."

"Can you type quickly?" she asked.

"Yes, I can, but why do you ask?"

"Well, Richard is really busy now and he's leaving in a car to catch a flight to Miami. I reckon you've got ten minutes to get a fax to me. Put it all down on a page and I promise you I'll make sure he brings it with him to read."

Yes, I could type quite fast with my two-fingers style. That wasn't the problem. I had presented my case many times to potential investors, suppliers of services and the regulatory authorities. I had written seven iterations of the business plan. Our executive summary alone ran to about six pages. I had ten minutes to encapsulate the whole deal plus what I wanted Branson to do in less than a page. I sent the fax.

Three weeks later I got a call from a guy in Virgin Atlantic Airways who said Richard had asked him to see me and could I get myself to London. I arrived at the Excelsior Hotel promptly at 12.30 to meet with Hugh Welburn. Hugh had been Richard Branson's aviation adviser from the start of his airline adventure. Having retired early from BA, Hugh brought with him not only a wealth of experience but also a high degree of innovative flair. He had invented the whole concept of apex fares in the early 1960s. He had been BA's first marketing manager for Concorde. He was a route economics expert. Not that Hugh had an intimidating style, but I quickly got the picture that I was in the presence of someone who had vastly more knowledge about this airline business than I would ever learn in a whole lifetime.

This was not a time to panic. Have confidence in your proposition, I told myself. I was invited to tell my story. The emphasis in the initial questioning was on my motivation rather than on the details of the plan. It was very apparent that Hugh was a man who actually saw the potential of success for any airline venture through the eyes of the ultimate arbitrator, the passenger. We were going to get along all right.

Not that I needed to fall back on props, but I was very glad I could drag from my bag a copy of a critique of our business plan which I had commissioned some months earlier from Professor Rigas Doganis of Cranfield University. Prof. Doganis carries weight in the world of aviation. It had personally cost me

stg£5,000 for the first iteration and another stg£3,000 for an up-
dated version, but it said we were serious enough to let ourselves
be second-guessed by the best. There would be more meetings
and within two weeks we were sitting down with Syd Pennington, an amiable Glaswegian who had recently been plucked from
Marks & Spencer to bring his commercial intuition to bear in his
new role as Managing Director of Virgin Atlantic. Syd was a
tough talker, straight and very fair.

Both Hugh and Syd were up for the idea of Cityjet operating
under a franchise of the Virgin brand. The plan was not complex.
Cityjet would have its aircraft painted in the Virgin livery with
the "Cityjet" logo prominently displayed on the forward fuselage.
Cityjet would work with Virgin to co-invent a customer service
appropriate to a short-haul flight and cabin crew selection together with training would have a heavy Virgin influence. All
Cityjet air crew and ground staff would wear the Virgin uniform.
Cityjet would also use the Virgin prefix of VS on all of its flights.
Ticketing and revenue collection would be undertaken on Virgin's
plates already in place with every travel agent in Ireland and the
UK. Virgin's reservation centre in London would handle all bookings for Cityjet while Cityjet would establish its own reservations
centre in Dublin for Irish-originating traffic. Virgin would not invest capital for an equity stake in Cityjet. However, Cityjet would
agree to pay a franchise fee which would be a negotiated percentage of gross revenue to cover all services provided by Virgin and
for the use of the brand.

We had come very far very fast with Virgin, but without the
man himself buying in to the concept, it would never fly. I was
told in plain terms by both Syd and Hugh that I had to do a number on Richard. "Go and see him one-on-one. If he likes you he'll
listen to the plan."

I knew I wasn't the first entrepreneur to grace the Branson
business bunker on Holland Park. A disarmingly charming set-up
greets you as you walk into what is a fantastic townhouse with an

enviable location. I immediately felt overdressed in my suit and tie, as people buzzed around in jeans and T-shirts. "Oh, hello. Richard's expecting you but he's doing an interview with Channel 4 right now. He shouldn't be too long. Coffee?"

Forty-five minutes later, he walked into the room carrying his own mug of coffee, sporting a fine suntan and dressed . . . well, I suppose "very casually" would best describe it. "Tell me about yourself," he invited in a hesitant, almost nervous tone. In the months that were to follow I would soon get to recognise this quasi-insecure or shy approach to speech as one of his trademarks and most definitely not a reliable indicator of where his brain was at in the moment.

I was face-to-face with my business icon. I was nervous but determined to get him on board. I had committed to this path now and there was no going back to the team in Dublin with a "no". I gave it everything. I suppose the passion I felt for this business adventure came through more than anything else. He warmed towards me. He certainly seemed to me to be getting excited at what I was trying to do. He picked up on the notion of giving Aer Lingus a bloody nose. They represented the establishment, a strong resonance perhaps with his bruising battles with British Airways. He was also taken with the idea of putting a brand new airport on the business map of London. If we were successful so too would be the airport. If Virgin was accredited with that success, then Virgin's image of a business airline of choice would be enhanced with the City "suits". A further spin-off might be leverage with City Airport and the prospects of launching more routes and becoming dominant in this market segment.

All of the above was mixed in with a certain empathy with my struggle to get this airline started. But he was engaged. I had his attention. Where to next? "You've got to bring my management team at the airline along with you on this one. Spend some time with them working out the details and then if we end up with a viable plan I'll look at it." That wasn't a "no". It wasn't a "yes" either but somehow I felt it was a whole lot better than the kind of "maybes" I was getting used to hearing over the past few months.

We had serious work to do with the Virgin management. I was amazed at how many of the most senior officers of the company got themselves involved in this process. The debates over many aspects of our business plan raged furiously. There was throughout this phase a very strong "anti" bias coming from a few people in the Virgin team. It was clear they didn't believe the brand should be franchised to us. There was already a franchise precedent: Virgin had an arrangement with a small Greek airline who were operating a daily flight from Gatwick to Athens in their colours and on their flight numbers. While the protagonists we were encountering seemed to be quite happy with the Greek operation, they were very opposed to helping us. They were not happy with the concept of London City Airport; they had no confidence in the viability of the route, etc., etc. It seemed as if they would latch onto anything that could be held up as a reason for not doing it.

Syd Pennington gave us a hard time in our discussions and he was instrumental in our making many alterations to the business plan. Overall, though, it was emerging that he believed it could work. Hugh Welburn also brought the weight of his experience to bear and while not agreeing with everything we wanted to do, was in very broad support that we could be successful. So it seemed that the threats from within the Virgin camp had been overcome and back we went to Richard for the royal determination.

We got the green light, subject to the satisfactory conclusion of a franchise agreement which would be drawn up by Virgin's lawyers, Hardbottle and Lewis. There were many occasions in the subsequent weeks when I felt a more apt name for the Virgin lawyers would be "Hardball, You Lose"!

In parallel with the unfolding story with Virgin, we continued to plough ahead with investor discussions. Fortunately, the three institutions we were talking to had a good relationship with each other, even though they competed fiercely for pension and investment business in Ireland. While we negotiated with the Dublin office of the Friends Provident and their investment director, Pramit Ghose, we also made a good few trips to Edinburgh to deal directly with John Lawrie of Scottish Provident and Des Doran of Standard Life. In fact, it was on one of those trips to see John Lawrie that the whole gig nearly ended. Permanently.

Luke and I flew into Edinburgh for a mid-morning meeting in Scottish Provident and we needed to make it back to Dublin for a meeting with the Norwich Union Investment Manager in the early afternoon. The problem was, the next flight out of Edinburgh was at teatime. Aer Lingus had a lunchtime flight from Glasgow that would do. We got into a black taxi and foolishly propositioned our very young driver that if he got us to Glasgow Airport within the hour there would a good tip in it for him. Black cabs are not noted for their acceleration but when you do get them up to speed, they are very good at holding it, probably because of the sheer weight of the beast. We came up the brow of a hill in the outside lane of the motorway and there we saw it: the back of a blue Ford Mondeo, the last in a line of stationary traffic straight ahead of us, growing larger and larger in the windscreen. Our driver's right foot went for the brake as Luke and I applied all four feet to the dividing wall behind the driver's seat.

The front of the cab finished where the back seat of the Mondeo had been. Miraculously, no one was even hurt. We got out of our greatly-reduced-in-length taxi and helped a very shaken commander to leave his turret. The guy in the Mondeo was OK but couldn't believe his good fortune that it was only metal on metal. Just then a young girl in a Volkswagen who happened to be in the line of stopped cars ahead of the Mondeo, enquired as to how everybody was. "You wouldn't be going past Glasgow Airport?" I asked. "Yes? Could you give us a lift?" I felt bad about the poor taxi driver and how he was going to explain this back at the ranch. We gave him £100 plus what we thought the fare would be. The traffic was moving again and we were in it in the Volkswagen

Golf. We ran past check-in as we knew it was useless to try to plead about trying to get on the flight. We flashed our tickets, not boarding passes, at security but were eventually apprehended at the boarding gate. In the ensuing confusion, the flight was held. We talked our way out of trouble and onto the flight. We got to the meeting with Norwich. It never amounted to anything in the end. We were beginning to behave like busy fools. Time to get a grip.

I felt we were very close to getting a positive decision out of at least one if not two of our institutions. I could really sense that the case had been well made and their very probing questions answered thoroughly. Behind the scenes they were conferring, which probably meant all or nothing. They decided they would make a collective leap of faith. We had three notably conservative financial institutions saying they were backing our fledgling start-up airline. This was incredible, especially against a background of Aer Lingus being given their last EU-permissible slug of State funding and the recent collapse of GPA, which had left many institutional investors licking their wounds.

More or less at the same time we got the nod from our private investors. I certainly clued them in on the emerging relationship with Virgin and it probably helped that I assured them that unless we could reach agreement with Virgin there was no point in launching the airline, as we would fail on our own to sell enough seats out of London.

So at last we were funded, but now the emphasis was on not slipping up with Virgin on the negotiation of the fine detail of the franchise agreement. Meanwhile, our tiny team was hard pressed, and to keep everything else on track we needed to hire some more people. We took on Peter Ribeiro, who had previously been General Manager of Stena Line in Ireland. Peter had also got prior experience with Jury's Hotels and the Irish Tourist Board. Peter's role was to implement a sales distribution strategy with the travel agents in Ireland.

In October, we were joined by Miriam Matthews, who would subsequently claim she never had a job description in her time with Cityjet but just got on with it. And "it" at the time was everything to do with co-ordinating the many bits that were going on and simply making us function in an organised way.

Kevin Barry was busy poaching a senior training pilot from Malmo Aviation who were operating BAe 146s on domestic routes in Sweden. But Malmo Aviation also flew a twice-a-day service from Bromma, Stockholm to London City. Malmo Aviation would go on to occupy more than a few chapters in this story, but at the time all of us were blissfully ignorant of what was to unfold. Anyway, Kevin was successful with his offer and we were joined by Chris Nielsen who set up our standard operating procedures (SOPs) which saved us an enormous amount in time and effort in inventing this from scratch. With this move, Kevin was not only buying in flight operations expertise on the BAe 146 but also on the very challenging short field of London City Airport.

Paddy O'Reilly was busy working out the details of a contract with Hunting Aircraft who would undertake all of our line maintenance and heavy maintenance under an arrangement to be approved by the Department of Transport.

BAe were pressing me to put down the deposits for the first two aircraft. We had agreed to take two aircraft coming out of service with Crossair. They were already fitted with blue leather seats and they had very adequate galleys. They were ideal for what we wanted. Their airframe times (hours of flying on the clock) were relatively low for six-year-old aircraft and our technical inspections indicated the aircraft were in good shape. At a monthly rental of US$120,000 per aircraft, BAe were seeking a deposit of US$720,000 to cover three months.

But learning how to live in the land of "Catch 22", I knew I could not release that kind of money before we were certain we had a "go" with Virgin, and there was still Hardbottle and Lewis with their franchise agreement to deal with. I stalled once again.

The "anti" faction in Virgin had a field day when it came to the franchise agreement. The document that the lawyers were instructed to draw up was ludicrously complex, lengthy, totally one-sided and completely uncommercial. There were intense rows across the table. Phones got slammed down. This was a disaster. I had arranged for Richard Branson to appear in late November on RTÉ's *The Late Late Show*, Ireland's and the world's longest-running live television chat show. The idea was to have Richard announce the forthcoming launch of Virgin Cityjet live to the nation on the most popular show on a Friday night.

It was five o'clock on that very same Friday and I was still in Hardbottle and Lewis. Having battled all day and conceded points I really didn't want to concede, the bullying was continuing. The people I was dealing with had just thrown in another grenade at the eleventh hour. This was crap. I stood up. I had to leave to catch a flight and be at Dublin Airport to meet Richard and bring him to the RTÉ TV studios. I also had arranged a celebratory party for after the show and invited all of our investors and our management team to be there to meet with Richard. I announced, "I don't agree. Once again you are being unreasonable. I'm leaving and we are on live TV in a few hours to announce the launch of the new airline. If you want to mess that up, then it's on your heads. Good luck."

I just made the flight. Our office was in the terminal building at Dublin. Luckily, it had a shower because I really needed one very badly. I was a mental wreck. I wasn't sure what would actually happen next. My colleagues were anxious to know what was going on. "The show is going on," I said, trying to sound confident. "Branson will be here in less than twenty minutes and we're going to the studios. Is everything sorted for afterwards?" — a very unnecessary question to ask of this team, partly on account of their super-efficiency but mostly because they loved parties.

There it was, this blue jumper coming down the escalator into the baggage hall. There was a swarm of well-wishers and autograph hopefuls in the wake of the blond, bearded people's champion. Aer Rianta, the airport authority, did their stuff and whisked him through the VIP corridor and out to the limousine we had organised. It was raining.

"We have a problem, Pat," he said over the din of what had instantly become a noisy car. Richard's children, Holly and Sam, were naturally vying for his attention as it was a Friday evening and no doubt there was some catching up to be done. Jane was talking with Joan, Richard's wife, and Pearse was looking at me to try to figure just how bad things might get.

"Frances Farrow [Virgin's in-house legal counsel at the time] says we can't conclude the agreement as there are some outstanding issues." I gave him my view of where we had got to at his lawyers' office and what my position was. He took on board what I said but he needed to phone Frances to talk it over. I asked the driver for his car phone. (This was late 1993 and mobiles were still a few short months away, unless you wanted to carry something half the size of a public telephone box around in your pocket.)

"It doesn't work very well in the car when its raining," responded our driver. "I'll pull over and Mr Branson will have to step outside to use it." The jumper was getting very wet as Richard stretched the cord on the phone to its limit as he attempted to talk to Frances on the side of the airport motorway. The line broke down about three times and he gave up, deciding to press ahead to the studio and use a land line from there. It was a struggle to keep the mood in the car upbeat for the next nine miles of wet city streets, but we didn't let it flag. Great team effort.

We dispensed with the niceties on arrival at the studio reception area and grabbed the first office with a phone we could find. The conversation was animated and certainly not going the way I wanted. He came off the call with a very downbeat look on his face. "I can't go against the advice I'm being given. I won't announce the launch of the airline. I'll just do a general interview with Gay."

I was too mad to be upset, if that makes sense. I was not going to have the efforts of good people evaporate through an intransigent stance on a non-commercial point in a legal agreement. I took a deep breath: "Richard, you and I both know what we are trying to accomplish here. We have an understanding that doesn't require such a one-sided and overly legalistic document to underpin what we are doing. You have the power to make the decision. Trust me. You are not increasing the exposure of Virgin or yourself over this issue. I will work to sort this out on Monday, but we have to go ahead tonight with this announcement."

There was a silence between us. There was an unease outside the glass-roomed office; Richard was wanted in make-up. The clock was ticking down to airtime. Heavy sighing led to the sound of words: "OK. OK. I'll take a chance I suppose. I can always . . . No, I'll do it. Let's do it."

He was brilliant. Gay Byrne, the legendary host of *The Late Late Show*, had interviewed him before and it was very clear they liked each other. Pearse and myself were sitting on steps at the side of the live audience gantry, as we gave up our seats to Rob and Anna, friends of Richard and Joan who had come from Kildare to be with them. In fairness to Richard, he tried to bring us into the picture, but Gay wasn't biting. Anyhow, out went the message, loud and clear. Virgin had done a deal with Cityjet. January would see the launch of an exciting alternative way of commuting to and from London.

We got to the restaurant. The investors and their partners were there along with selected guests from the travel trade and of course the slowly but steadily growing Cityjet community. Branson worked the room. The atmosphere was electric and the party had no difficulty in taking off. I didn't know whether to laugh or cry. Very few in that high-spirited room had any idea how close we had come to switching to a wake. I was exhausted. Monday would approach fast. This is mad.

Chapter Four

WE CAN'T BE STOPPED NOW, CAN WE?

M onday came. The going wasn't easy but we got everybody comfortable around the franchise agreement over the course of the week. And there the challenges to getting started should have ended. But, like so often with the Cityjet adventure, just as you thought you were cleared for take-off, another obstacle would be placed on the runway.

The pace was gathering as we had only eight weeks to our first scheduled flight. The recruiting had been going well and the co-operation we were getting from the Virgin cabin services training department was fantastic. They sent two of their senior managers to live with us in Dublin to help organise the crew selection. Our joint Cityjet/Virgin interview panel did an incredible job, and I believe the calibre of our initial intake of thirty cabin crew was outstanding and was to prove to be one of the key factors in setting us apart from our competition.

On the pilot front, we were attracting a good mix of experienced BAe 146 captains and talented young first officers with the capability to convert to type successfully. One of the precious few advantages of a recession for a start-up airline is the availability of good pilots and we exploited it to the hilt.

By early November, the cabin crew training was near completion, the deposits for the aircraft were paid, pilot conversion was nearly complete and the engineering side of the house was coming together. The design of the actual in-flight product had been concluded and we were in test mode with the catering experts in Virgin and the out-sourced contracting companies who would prepare the on-board meals to this specification. In addition, we had made huge strides in getting our marketing lined up and we had taken on more people to cover sales and reservations.

It was again a Friday when one of the most dedicated of the Virgin "anti" brigade succeeded in getting to Branson with his view that our business plan just didn't stack up on his latest set of calculations. I was returning late that evening from yet another of my three or four trips a week to the UK to work on another piece of the jigsaw when I heard the news that Richard was about to call the whole thing off and withdraw the franchise. My disbelief turned to rage quickly enough.

The next morning, being a Saturday, I phoned Richard at his home in Oxford. I probably sounded like John McEnroe in his customary Wimbledon outburst, which always began with "you cannot be serious". I painted the reality of the picture of what exactly had been going on over recent weeks. Young Irish cabin crew halfway through their training with Virgin in London. The market in Dublin and the expectation that had been created around the new Virgin/Cityjet venture. Not for the first time did I find Richard unsure and uncertain about his position. But there was a consistency emerging here about his reluctance to go against his lieutenants. It was a tough conversation and I was like an Exocet missile that would not give up on homing in on my target. Richard stumbled and stuttered his way through the exchange and finished by suggesting that all of his people with a view and all of ours should convene on Monday evening at Holland Park to give it one more go.

It was a tense and miserable weekend. I really felt this could be it. I probably always had a sense of the animosity towards our project from certain people within Virgin. I was always worried about how they might spike us and this was looking awfully like they had pulled it off. I galvanised support from anywhere it might count. I called Robin Southwell in BAe and asked him to attend the Holland Park meeting. The rest of our management team bid us farewell late on that Monday afternoon in late November as Luke, who was giving a massive amount of time in his unremunerated role as non-executive chairman, together with Pearse and myself, headed for our deciding encounter in London. This was a cup final and there was no prize for second.

The meeting got going around 7.30 that evening and we were seated at an enormously long table in what was once most probably a stately dining room in this beautiful house on Holland Park. The antagonists put forward their case that they felt the whole scheme was simply unviable and that Virgin should disassociate itself immediately. Robin Southwell from BAe put up a strong counter-view which fundamentally endorsed the arguments we were putting on the table throughout the course of the evening. To their great credit, Syd Pennington and Hugh Welburn in their own individual styles came down heavily in favour of honouring Virgin's commitment to the venture and left everyone in the room in no doubt of their intolerance of the arguments being advanced by some of their Virgin colleagues. Then, as always, it was up to Richard.

He stumbled quite a bit through his opening remarks but clearly demonstrated a good grasp of the challenges some of his people anticipated. I still couldn't call it as to which way he was going to go, when suddenly he declared that, having listened to all who spoke, he was going to put his trust in the venture. That was it. The relief on our side of the table was massive. A victory for now definitely, but we had left some wounded well capable of re-grouping for another day. I knew we were always going to have to watch our backs.

It was now about ten o'clock. I phoned Jane to tell her the news. Next it was the anxious bunch in the office in Dublin. "We have an airline" seemed to be the only appropriate words I could use to convey the outcome. Finally I called my Dad, who had been sharing the unfolding drama of the past eighteen months through my Sunday morning updates. This was a Monday and this development couldn't wait until next Sunday. It was hopelessly late for a flight and we had not booked ourselves a hotel. Syd ordered a taxi and insisted we were going to his house for a beer and a bed. Together with his wife Annie, we savoured the moment in their kitchen before crashing out for a fitful sleep.

Now we had a clear run-in ahead of us to get the airline in the air. The deadline of 10 January for our first scheduled flight was going to be upon us in no time. But we were getting into gear, with our staff numbers now at about eighty-five. Our marketing strategy was beginning to look practical. In Dublin, we would have control of how we went about winning market share and in London, Virgin would use their well-proven formula for getting noticed. Our marketing team had been bolstered by the hiring of Sharon Ryan from 98 FM, Dublin's most successful commercial radio station. We had signed one of Dublin's leading advertising agencies following a competitive bid process. The media space was booked, the creative looking truly innovative and the press were being made curious around this imminent David and Goliath battle on the Dublin/London route.

The final act in obtaining our AOC from the Department of Transport was the placing of the aircraft on the Irish register. This could only be done following an inspection by the Department of Transport of the aircraft prior to release to Cityjet by BAe. There was a considerable amount of work to be completed on the aircraft and it was looking like the actual date of hand-over of the first plane would be 23 December. This was very tight; should anything slip, we would be into the Christmas holidays, which meant no service from parts vendors and skeleton staff on duty at the Hunting Aircraft maintenance facility in East Midlands, where the aircraft was being prepared. To compound the pressure we had also undertaken to perform two Christmas charter flights to Malaga.

Meanwhile, we had a few weeks to sweat things when a quite unique marketing opportunity came our way. There was a very high-profile story running on Sky and other British news channels about the plight of four Britons who were being held as "hostages" by Saddam Hussein in Baghdad. Ted Heath, the former British Prime Minister, had taken up their cause and was campaigning for their release. I was in a telephone conversation with Will Whitehorn, Branson's media manager. We were talking about the need for some pre-launch publicity stunt when he brought up the Iraq hostages situation. "When will your aircraft be painted and ready to fly?" he asked. I should have known what was coming next, given Will's reputation for the daring media coups he had pulled off for Branson in the past. "Oh, not for another three weeks or so," I said. "Pity," said Will, "Richard is of a mind to try and do something about those hostages in Iraq." "Will, let me call you back on this," I said, burning up with excitement at what was going through my head.

I dived for Robin Southwell's number at BAe. "Robin have you got a flyable 146 lying around anywhere right now?" "Dunno, I suppose we must have. What are you thinking about?" he asked. I outlined the conversation with Whitehorn and put it to him that if we could grab a serviceable 146, paint it in the Virgin Cityjet scheme, crew it with Cityjet cabin crew and find two qualified British-licensed pilots (as we had no AOC yet), we could go off and be heroes in the full gaze of the media. Good for Virgin, great for Cityjet, profiling the 146 as a can-do aircraft and bringing the hostages home. "If Branson pays for the paint job and the fuel I'll get you an aircraft," he told me.

I rationalised this seemingly cynical act of opportunism on the basis that what Saddam was doing was all about media manipulation and the exploitation of these Britons. The fact was, someone, somehow was going to bring those unfortunate people, who were being used as pawns, home. Branson had publicly said he was concerned, so why not make it happen and benefit from the publicity in the process. Saddam was playing a media game with the hostages as the pawns. He had announced that they would be re-leased at a certain time and we set out to have an aircraft arrive there to coincide with that time.

We had three days to pull this off. Kevin Barry organised the sourcing of the two British pilots and he declared he was going on the trip also. We picked the cabin crew from the two dozen or so who volunteered and Syd Pennington joined the team, bringing with him a large wedge of cash just in case there were places and officials along the lengthy trip that needed lubricating.

The paint was barely dry as the aircraft took off for Brindisi, on the toe of Italy, for its first refill. The coverage was enormous with the Virgin and Cityjet logos in full view and, as you would expect, Branson appearing on TV screens everywhere for the two days of the unfolding saga.

So, in theory, Cityjet's first operational flight was actually deep into Iraq. In Dublin, the papers picked up on it and so we had achieved our pre-launch publicity coup on both sides of the Irish Sea. The boost for staff morale was big, because nerves had been fraying as we edged closer to launch and still had no aircraft to call our own.

To keep staff on an upbeat tempo we decided we would hold the inaugural Cityjet Christmas party. It was fitting for me, I sup-pose, to choose the Wanderers Clubhouse at Lansdowne Road, an intimate little building, as the venue. Jane set about creating a wonderful atmosphere with her decorative skills and her eye for colour. She also booked a phenomenal band called Loudest Whis-per, got the catering sorted and we had an incredible night.

Come 23 December and Kevin Barry, Pearse, chief engineer Paddy O'Reilly and myself arrived at Hunting Aircraft in East Mid-lands. There was a lot of paperwork to be completed with both BAe and Hunting, and the inspector from the Department of Transport was finalising his work. Robin Southwell and Graham Whitmarsh of BAe presented me with a model of the 146 in our livery with a

cryptic inscription which showed many scratched out dates for delivery — a humorous poke at my stalling tactics of the past few
months.

And then we were all of a sudden free to go and take our aircraft with us back to Dublin. Our newly hired Chief Pilot Phil Bar-
raball was in the left-hand seat with Kevin performing the co-pilot
duties. I was like a six-year-old sitting in the jump seat, daring to
believe what we were doing here. As we overflew the airport road
on short finals into Dublin, Jane was driving right underneath us
as she made her way out to meet us, and had a perfect view of our
gleaming paint job. It was a wonderful homecoming and so confident were we on the day that we had deliberately bought one-
way tickets to the UK. We were coming home on Cityjet.

The next morning I dragged myself from my bed. It was
Christmas Eve. I was tired and possibly hung-over after the wel-
coming home drinks and the christening of EI-JET, our firstborn. I
met Paddy O'Reilly at the office and we waited by the fax. Paddy
had arranged with John Nolan, the Director of Airworthiness at
the Department of Transport, to have the registration of the aircraft on the Irish register formalised and to then personally issue
our AOC. By eleven o'clock, we had it.

Going into that Christmas Day, it was a time to look back over
the previous eighteen months or so. We had got our funding. We
had secured a strategic partnership with Virgin. We had our licence. We had crew and staff. We had an aircraft, with another
one due on 2 January. All we needed now was passengers, and
loads of them. We selected our guest list for the inaugural flight
(which in actual fact would be the second flight — we needed to
centre things around Branson, and he could not make it to Dublin
the night before).

So the first actual scheduled flight departed out of Dublin at
7.15 am and on board were a handful of fare-paying passengers, a
load of journalists, Kevin Barry at the controls and myself working the press. On arrival at LCY there was a fantastic welcome

from Bill Charnock and his management team, with a large gathering of journalists. Branson was such a draw. There he was in yet another jumper and a huge grin. We posed for shots, gave a TV interview and got on board and off to Dublin on the return.

At Dublin Airport's VIP centre, we convened our press conference. Our guest of honour was Charlie McCreevy, the Minister for Tourism and Trade. He did us proud. Branson charmed his audience and I said my few words. The photo opportunities were excellent but were not proofed against the infamous Dublin wit. While the Minister, Branson and myself were lining up for yet another shot with the aircraft in the background, an Aer Lingus maintenance man passing by was heard to say, "What sort of a clown would call his new aircraft 'eijet'?" (the aircraft's registration was in fact EI-JET and the word "eejit" is local terminology for idiot!)

All our guests boarded the flight and, led by Head of Cabin Crew, Linda Corr, were treated to a fantastic demonstration of what lay in store for our new passengers. Lunch followed in The Tower Thistle where there were several local dignitaries and MPs, more speeches, and then back to the aircraft once more. We had arranged for a staff party that night in Dublin to mark the kick-off of what everybody had been working so hard to achieve. Richard was supposed to be otherwise engaged that evening but nothing would do him but to come back to Dublin with us for the party. We left Lilly Bordello's at about half past. I had had a twenty-two-hour day and yet I didn't feel like I could sleep much; I was anxious to see what the critics had to say in the morning papers.

Chapter Five

WELCOME TO REAL LIVE FLYING

I could not have predicted what was on those front pages. "TRAFFIC TANGLE SNARLS AIRLINE RACE: *Cityjet, the new Irish airline, took off yesterday and immediately ran into flak when it lost the first round of the big London air race against Aer Lingus.*"

Our whole marketing thrust was predicated on saving businesspeople time in making the trip to and from the City of London. We argued that flying into a tiny airport meant only five minutes from touchdown to being in the back of a cab, compared to twenty-five minutes through Heathrow. We promised it would only take twenty-five minutes to the City given average traffic conditions, compared to fifty minutes on the Piccadilly Line from Heathrow.

What we were completely unaware of until we read it in the papers was that the Rotherhithe Tunnel had suffered a partial collapse on the very morning of our first flight. This threw the traffic system in East London into complete chaos and delays of up to two hours were being experienced on the way to the City. Also unknown to us was that there were two *Irish Independent* journalists, in a race between the airlines, using Cityjet to London City Airport and Aer Lingus to Heathrow. The latter got to Oxford Street some seventy minutes ahead of the Cityjet passenger.

To compound the matter, later in the morning someone from marketing burst into my office to tell me to listen to the Pat Kenny radio programme on RTÉ. I caught the tail-end of the interview with the very same journalist who had been beaten by his colleague by the now famous seventy minutes to Oxford Street. He praised the service, the crew, the lovely leather seats with superior leg room, the fantastic City airport, but oh what a shame about the traffic into town! He went on to suggest, live on air to the nation, that businesspeople should perhaps give Cityjet a miss for about four months when the tunnel would be fixed, and then it would work. The kiss of death in an instant.

I phoned the RTÉ studios and demanded to speak to Pat Kenny. I got through to the producer. "Listen," I said, "you can't leave things like this. This is a killer blow for us. Have you any idea the damage this simple suggestion that businesspeople should give Cityjet a miss for a few months will do to us?" I shouted down the phone. "I want a re-match, and not in a few months but before this week is out. This time include every airline flying Dublin to London and every London Airport." Pat Kenny couldn't resist this type of live radio drama and so the great London Air Race was set for the coming Friday. RTÉ would muster five journalists who would each fly with one of the five airlines (Aer Lingus, British Midland, British Airways, Ryanair and Cityjet) to one of the five London airports (Heathrow, Gatwick, Stansted, Luton and London City).

The offending tunnel would not be fixed for weeks but we were counting on the fact that those people who had suffered most in that awful traffic jam would work out alternative routes to avoid spilling onto the principal way into the City from Docklands. We also had to make sure we would not get an air traffic slot delay from our scheduled first flight of the morning at 7.15. I was nervous of potential "dirty tricks" in the form of priority being shown to more established operators. Then there was the ever-present risk of a technical snag with the aircraft inducing a delay. To cover that one, we had the comfort of a second scheduled departure at 07.55; if disaster struck, we would do a rapid transfer of passengers to the second aircraft, which would already have its catering loaded on-board early. We sweated our way to race day. In between, we planned major adjustments to our advertising campaign, which would now switch to "We've proved we're the fastest option to London". All we needed now was a significant victory over all-comers to make the claim stick.

Friday morning, I was in the flight ops room at 6.00 am. Kevin Barry was going to be on the flight deck and he was busy filing plans and looking for any obvious early signs of slot delays. Paddy O'Reilly was with the line engineers contracted from Hunting Aircraft with a view to delivering a rapid response to any technical problems should bad luck strike. Miriam Matthews was there to assist our check-in and boarding staff should there be any mishap such as a missing passenger with a checked bag in the hold. Apart from washing the windscreen again and kicking the tyres, there was nothing left to do. We launched exactly on time. From that point on, there was nothing we could do to influence the outcome except for lighting a few thousand candles. We landed at London City slightly ahead of schedule and "our competing journalist" was observed walking out the door to the taxi and coach area five minutes after touchdown. We were now at the mercy of the traffic. The radio show came on at 9.00 and Pat Kenny promised regular updates on the Great Air Race as despatches from his intrepid travellers filtered through. Comfortably before ten o'clock, it was all over. Our passenger had arrived at the designated spot in Oxford Street and there was not a sign of any of the others. It was a full hour before the Aer Lingus "jockey" came past the post, with the British Midland effort some twenty minutes or so further back. Ryanair and Stansted was next, with BA Cityflyer and Gatwick and Ryanair again with Luton bringing up the rear some two hours later.

In fairness to Pat Kenny and his crew, he really made noise on the day about our fantastic win and the message went out loud and clear that Cityjet was the fastest way to London. The next days saw our cheeky ads in the media boasting about our win and putting our advantage in terms of speed and convenience squarely in front of people.

The next few weeks were critical in getting Cityjet on the radar of companies who had a lot of their executives travelling back and forth to London. If it was as easy as asking the CEO or Financial Director of a company to support us, then we would have been confident of getting our revenue targets pretty quickly. Shaking hands at the top does not translate into airline seats being purchased by the company's staff. There were personal assistants and secretaries who took care of travel for management and in the majority of cases they would use the services of a travel agent. So even if we felt we could count on the goodwill of a company, the travel agent still had the power to place the business. In the Dublin business community in 1994, when you said you wanted to fly to London, this would almost always result in a travel agent booking their client to Heathrow. We had a lot of educating to do.

I was particularly anxious not to scare off any passengers who had the potential to become regular flyers with us. The approach into City Airport has to be flown at a steep angle of attack and to the uninitiated the exaggerated nose-down attitude can be noticeable. I had this idea of creating a sense of involvement for passengers in this exciting adventure of putting a jet airliner down on what used to a wharf in London's Docklands. I spoke to Kevin Barry about the prospect of his crews allowing the cockpit door to remain open during flight especially so that passengers could witness a bird's-eye view of the postage stamp of a runway growing larger in the windscreen during the final descent. It worked really well for us, becoming a talking-point and valuable word-of-mouth referral tool in the business community. Of course, those days of passengers leaning their heads into the aisle to get a view of what's going on in the "office" up-front are sadly no more after 9/11.

Getting travel agents on side was about money. Aer Lingus in particular were paying way above the standard 9 per cent commission. We had to go as high as 15 per cent to keep pace and have a reasonable chance of agents pushing our service to their clients. On-line web-based booking engines were a long way off in 1994. The agents just could not be bypassed, but had to be seduced and incentivised, and even then their allegiance was influenced by the commission aggregation deals on offer from airlines who operated a far more extensive route network than the fledgling Cityjet. There was no easy way through this. We built relationships with senior executives of user companies, their internal people who arranged travel and the agents who actually arranged the ticketing. We formed a secretaries' club and ran a frequent bookers scheme, where we awarded points every time they booked their boss with Cityjet. We converted the points into tangible prizes like cosmetics, clothes, concert tickets and dinner-for-two vouchers. We attracted some 400 members to the secretaries' club in our first year.

We used radio advertising extensively, with very provocative messages delivered in a tasteful style. I worked on building the image of the airline as one of a businessperson's airline set up by businesspeople. I accepted every invitation I got to speak at business functions organised by various institutes and associations. My schoolboy interest in debating was paying dividends now.

Meanwhile, the management of the relationship with Virgin was proving to be difficult. There was an insatiable appetite on their part for a lot of meetings, which were nearly always held in Crawley. Within the first few weeks of operation, Virgin spent an enormous amount of our UK advertising budget. The early results of this activity were not washing through in terms of seats purchased out of London. In spite of this, we endured inane meetings about the protection of the Virgin brand rather than focusing on how they would sell more seats for us, as per our deal. The performance of the Virgin reservations centre for Cityjet was awful. In many cases, when people rang up they were told emphatically by Virgin reservations agents that Virgin didn't fly to Dublin.

On the positive side, we were getting on famously with Virgin's cabin crew training department and it was very evident that we had the finest crew on short-haul flying in Britain or Ireland. Equally, our relationship with Virgin's in-flight catering planners was very good and we had succeeded in delivering a superb product for our passengers. It was, however, costing us a fortune, especially as we had launched with a single-class cabin. This meant that people who travelled in the back on cheaper restricted fares also enjoyed this very high-quality cuisine. This sparked one of our first rows with Virgin. We wanted to revisit what we gave to whom consistent with the fares passengers were paying. Certain people in Virgin dug in and cited the protection of the brand as the reason for not agreeing to alter the service.

This argument dragged on for three months or more, at a huge cost to Cityjet. We finally got our way but at another enormous cost. Richard Branson, on learning that Sir Michael Bishop of British Midland had introduced a very low fare (for the time) at stg£69 return in economy class on Dublin/Heathrow immediately pressed us to match it. We were opposed to following Bishop. We were confident that our route was different and could carry a higher fare than Heathrow, even for economy passengers. But with Richard, it was almost a personal thing not to be undercut by anyone, even Sir Michael with whom he seemed to have a very good commercial relationship.

Now the increasingly defensive sales people in Virgin were latching on to the perfect reason why they had not sold more seats: price. We relented and agreed to the £69 economy fare. As a quid pro quo, Virgin allowed us to bring in a two-tier in-flight service. But there was even more sales rescue initiative to come from the marketing experts in Virgin. "You must have an early morning flight out of London City," they reasoned. This was daft thinking. Our counter-argument was based on the simple principle that any route is based on people favouring airports nearest their homes if an early start is contemplated. London City Airport was very convenient to where our target market in London worked, not where they lived. In fact, our whole marketing strategy for the London-originating business people was to encourage them to maintain their everyday routine of getting to their office, open the post and catch a mid-morning or lunchtime flight to Dublin. Alternatively, do a half or even whole day's work and catch an evening flight to Dublin, where our research had shown that UK businesspeople were more disposed to an overnight away than were their Irish counterparts. Splitting our two aircraft to perform an early morning service in both directions also meant we would be halving our peak-time capacity out of Dublin, where we were winning the business. The added burden of paying for the overnight expenses and arranging line maintenance cover at City Airport further upped the revenue target to make sense out of this move. Again, against our better judgement, we deferred to the supposedly superior experience of Virgin and committed to the changed schedule.

To supplement our flying activity on Dublin/London City, we negotiated a IR£3 million charter deal to operate on Saturdays and Sundays to Malaga and Faro from Dublin. Although the price we were getting per flight was not hugely profitable, the additional utilisation of the aircraft would make a very meaningful contribution towards our fixed overheads. We were now up to optimal aircraft usage for our fleet of two jets.

We were a few weeks beyond our first three months of operational flying when lightning struck in the form of an engine suffering what is termed a "catastrophic failure" in-flight over the Bay of Biscay en route to Faro. The significance of the timing lay in the fact that we had a three-month warranty on each of the four engines on-wing on each aircraft. After that, we were on our own should we suffer any major technical mishap. It shouldn't have been that way, particularly as the engine manufacturer, Textron Lycoming, had a special insurance-type programme known as Engine Maintenance Cost Protection (EMCP). By paying a set rate of US$52 per engine hour to the manufacturer, the cost liability for any significant damage to an engine would be carried by Textron. There was one problem from a Cityjet perspective. Textron insisted that an operator had to have a minimum of four aircraft to qualify for participation in EMCP. At two units, we were a little short.

Anyway, the aircraft had to return to Dublin with a blown engine. But that's why we carried a spare one in a box in our spares store. It had come from Crossair, where it had been overhauled in their manufacturer-approved repair facility. The paperwork seemed fine to the engineers. An engine change using a "raw engine" — that is, one in a box with none of the plumbing and accessories fitted — takes fourteen hours on a BAe 146. The guys worked hard through the night and the aircraft was serviceable by mid-morning on Sunday, in time for a charter flight.

Lightning does strike twice and, as I was to find out in Cityjet's case, it can strike many times. That perfectly good engine, exactly one hour into its flight, went bang: another catastrophic failure in the hot section, with the fallout of the damage being contained by the reinforced casing doing the job it was designed to do. We learned a lot about the seal in the No. 2 oil bearing on the ALF 502 engine that weekend. While the first engine failing with a lot of component life left to run was a bad break, the second such incidence of the same failure in an engine certified as completely overhauled and ready for another tour of duty on the wing was scarcely imaginable. And then the recriminations began to fly.

The focus was on the paperwork for the engine that came in the box from Crossair. Our contracted engineers from Hunting were adamant that there were no prescriptive tests to be done once the engine was fitted to the wing, apart from the mandatory engine run-ups to full and sustained power. Crossair were sticking to their position that the paperwork accompanying the engine made it patently clear that a "scavenger bearing" temperature reading should have been performed before declaring the engine fit for service. The fact that such a test could only be performed at a manufacturer-approved engine repair facility, and certainly not at an operator's line maintenance base should have sealed the matter, but it didn't.

The legal row was to drag on for all of two more years before a settlement was arrived at through arbitration, with Hunting, BAe, Crossair and Cityjet sharing the cost of the repair plus the rental payments on a replacement engine for all of that time. We had no change out of IR£0.5 million on this episode, plus a further IR£0.7 million bill for the first engine. My latest new priority was to get our engines qualified for participation for EMCP, as we couldn't contemplate such exposure going forward. Textron were going to have to change their restrictive rules.

During these first four months, I was also engaged in a small sideshow of trying to off-load the three SIAI Marchetti SF 260s that I had been stuck with. To get some movement and to reduce my bank borrowings, I finally got one away to a successful businessman in Newcastle who was also an aviation aficionado.

I dropped US$100,000 on the price but I needed to get some movement on resolving my problem. In spite of appalling weather, I found the ferry flight in the Marchetti with Kevin Barry alongside me a happy respite from what had all-too-fast become a pressure-cooker environment, with fresh challenges presenting themselves almost by the hour. Getting the airline into the air had been a very tough number. I was realising that keeping it there was going to be far harder.

I should have seen it coming. I allowed myself to get distracted through being sucked into every dogfight going as we entered the month of May, our fifth month of operations. Cash was very tight. Revenue was down on target due to passenger loads not being quite where we wanted them and there was downward pressure on our yield due to competitive action. But the real runaway train was costs. The in-flight service, which was receiving rave reviews, was expensive to produce. The new idea of overnighting an aircraft with crew in London was a heavy drain and worst of all was the battle every month to get our cash on time from Virgin. As we were using Virgin flight numbers and all ticketing was being done on Virgin's plates with travel agents in both the UK and Ireland, the airline clearing system known as Bank Settlement Plan (BSP) collected the money for flights and remitted it to Virgin. It was getting progressively more difficult to get this money — our money — released. Yes, under the terms of our franchise agreement, Virgin had a right to deduct payment in respect of services such as the shares reservations system we used, the nine per cent commission on sales made by Virgin's direct reservations in the UK, the franchise fee of four per cent of gross revenue, the crediting of frequent flyer miles to regular passengers and also a charge for overseeing the catering services. But the net balance should have been given to us without an intense amount of telephone dialogue and a protracted reconciliation exercise every month.

There was one particular guy in Virgin who seemed to take it on himself to second-guess our financial projections on almost a daily basis. Behind the scenes, there were noises being made about our financial robustness. While we were increasingly anxious about our ever-tightening cash position, I began to worry that the slowness in payments of our ticket revenue could unwittingly present Virgin with the means of finding themselves in the position of preferred creditor.

As part of our high-energy drive to win our target share of the business market in Dublin, I requested Richard Branson to come over on the first Friday in May to do a series of publicity appearances, starting with a high-profile lunch with the top travel agents and their selected main clients at the Berkeley Court Hotel. As usual, I met him in person off the plane and we went into the office where, having done his thing of making everybody feel wonderful, he told me he was getting worrying signals from one of his people over our increasingly precarious cash state and our forward revenue projections. I called in Teresa Racklyeft, our finan-

cial controller, to get her views on the cross-channel dialogue going on between the Virgin accountant and herself. It was obvious
that the intensity of the interaction between the two accountants
had increased significantly in the previous twenty-four hours,
which was beginning to look like a disastrous coincidence with
Branson's publicity mission.

It was showtime. I drove Richard to the Berkeley Court. He
spent a fair bit of time on the phone to the Virgin accountant.
Branson was getting edgy. He didn't like the prospect of a public
appearance against the backdrop of a potential meltdown in the
commercial relationship. He spoke to me about giving coded
warnings to his audience that all might not be as well as it should
be with the finances of Cityjet at this time. I was shocked. I could
scarcely believe that this famed street fighter, who had become
the underdog's business champion, was looking for the emergency exit even before there was the smell of smoke. But I had
seen him like this before. Back in November — was that only
seven months ago? — in the limo on the way to *The Late Late
Show*, he was being unnerved by someone at the other end of the
phone just as he was about to meet his public and give them news
of a bold new venture.

I was strong and clear: I told him that under no circumstances
was there going to be any discussion in public about Cityjet's financial position. I expected him to fulfil a commitment he had
made to me to re-kindle interest and enthusiasm for what we had
started and to encourage key influencers, in the form of the top
travel agents, to push more business our way.

The lunch was a huge success and yet again, in spite of his
misgivings and insecurity about the situation, Richard was a pro.
A hasty informal press briefing with a couple of selected journalists was followed by a dash in my car to RTÉ for an appearance on
the Ronan Collins radio show. Along the way, the Virgin man on
the phone was present with us once more as he planted fresh
seeds of doubt in Richard's head. I was busy too, talking to Teresa

back in the office to produce figures which would counter the ever-changing line of attack being put forward by her counterpart in Virgin. The radio show was a low-key affair, with Branson steering the chat to his involvement in the music business and staying safely away from questions about airlines.

Back into the car and more phone calls with Virgin and Teresa. Next stop was the Virgin Megastore where he wanted to do a walkabout. He bought two kids a video game each which they had their eyes on, but true to form he had no cash or cards and ended up signing an IOU for the store manager! The Shelbourne Hotel and the 400 members of the Cityjet secretaries club beckoned us for six o'clock. The place was buzzing. He was mobbed going in the front door and for the first time, I actually got a glimpse of what going out in public is like for a rock star. He was good. He gave away prizes of free tickets to faraway Virgin destinations. He created an incredible party atmosphere. This was more like it but I couldn't enjoy it. There was a sombre overhang in the air that only I knew anything about. *Smile. Don't let people see your discomfort.* I knew we were in deep trouble. The Virgin link was on the point of being sabotaged. It was too early to go it alone: they had the reservations system; they controlled our distribution; they collected our cash. There could be no orderly walking away to make alternate arrangements without a fresh capital injection. *How I broke up with Branson within six months* was hardly the ideal story to tell shareholders when you want more money.

And the day wasn't over yet. One more gig to do. Back to the Berkeley Court where we had arranged for him to do a fleeting appearance at the Irish travel journalists' dinner. Again, this was an almost exclusively female audience where our boy was a winner once more.

Richard sat in the back of my well-travelled BMW 535 with Jane sitting beside me as I drove to Kildare to deliver to Rob and Anna their fourth member of the Branson family taking up residence as their weekend house guests. Richard was tired, not from the appearances but I believe from a genuine worry that things might be coming to an end. I didn't try to argue that our financial position was strong because it wasn't. But there were very specific reasons for this. The performance of Virgin in terms of delivering revenue on the UK side was pretty poor. In Dublin we were doing well. I let him know I was deeply suspicious about the motives of the man from Virgin who peppered our day with incremental updates on his view of our financial well-being. I told him I thought it was gratuitously unfair to focus energy on the potential negative publicity fall-out for Virgin from a failed franchised arrangement to the exclusion of any meaningful effort to help turn things around. In my view, I felt that his man was advocating the provisioning of the lifeboat without anyone in Virgin lifting a finger to fix the hole in the side of the ship, which was eminently patchable. By mutual nod, we parked the conversation with Richard suggesting that we get everybody together in Crawley first thing Monday. Meanwhile, he wanted us to have a drink with him when we got to Rob and Anna's and to come over and spend Sunday with his family there. We did. We had a good time and I beat him at tennis. Once more, another Monday promised obscurity or deliverance.

Chapter Six

SETTING FIRE TO MONEY

We met in Crawley on Monday morning. Richard was there, as were Syd Pennington, Hugh Welburn and others, including he who had spent all of Friday in Richard's ear, courtesy of my car phone. We got the concerns around our cash position on the table and we looked at how revenue could be driven up in the short term and also how alleviation on cost could be achieved. I acknowledged that more capital was needed to be injected into the airline quickly. However, to get shareholder support we would have to show a high degree of self-help in the form of re-negotiated terms from major suppliers of the high cost items such as the aircraft manufacturers, the airport and maybe even Virgin.

We admitted that we were losing a ton of money. We had budgeted on losses for the first year but not at this rate of hemorrhage. We acknowledged the right for people in Virgin to be concerned at our trading position but what we needed was constructive help and not "I told you so, Richard" type of stuff coming from the "experts" in his employ.

There is the inescapable fact that the fixed costs that come with an airline infrastructure are huge. The only source of revenue for an airline is ticket sales on flights which in themselves incur considerable costs to operate. The challenge of course is to make sure there is sufficient flying activity with enough fare-paying passengers paying a decent level of fare to make the sums come out the right way at the end of every day. The whole rationale for getting into bed with Virgin in the first place was to secure a reasonable slice of the business market in London. Part of offering a Virgin-branded product to this market segment was an incredibly high specification in on-board service. This cost huge money. Virgin's marketing effort was failing to deliver the "suits" out of London on our flights and they were concentrating on selling low-priced fares to the leisure market predominantly.

For each flight launched with a less-than-adequate load factor, in terms of the number of passengers on-board, the books get harder to balance. But this wasn't where our problem lay because our passenger loads were quite good. Where we were losing money, however, was on our average fare yields. For each flight with an average yield (the fare being paid) that was lower than target, the more catching up of revenue has to be done on subsequent flights. Our projections prior to commencing operations indicated certain load factors and average fare yields. While we were very close to the numbers of passengers we set out to carry by this stage, the average fare we were achieving was lower. Compounding our problems was the fact that our direct operating costs of flights were higher than anticipated. To have a dependency on just two aircraft and one route to carry an undershoot in revenue and an overshoot in operating costs, together with paying for the huge fixed costs of the infrastructure, was a daunting task. We were burning about £130,000 in losses a week at this stage. We needed two things: more cash to stay in the race and more aircraft and more routes to spread the fixed costs of the airline infrastructure. In short, we had to stay in business to reach a point of critical mass.

This was my first real attempt at encouraging Virgin to see themselves more as partners in this venture rather than just as rent collectors who expected bad news and were determined to hold enough of our money to protect themselves from a bad debt. It was a risky stance but a large dose of reality was needed in the light of the proportional culpability of Virgin in the current plight of Cityjet. Some things got resolved speedily. The embarrassment of some in the room around the complete failure of the early-morning flight out of London City, demanded some weeks earlier by the Virgin marketing tigers, ensured no opposition to common sense being restored to our schedule of flights. The delay in introducing a lower-cost in-flight service for economy class was acknowledged as having cost us dearly and the two-tier in-flight service model was endorsed for immediate introduction.

Without anybody really saying *I do*, the marriage vows were renewed by default. No break-up yet, but what we might have called a victory some months earlier, we now would sensibly classify as not much above a relieving kick to touch. Those who wanted blood would not go away. They would just wait a little longer.

I was immediately catapulted back into fund-raising mode, a state of being I was destined to remain in unrelentingly for the rest of this story. But before I could approach shareholders and potential new investors, I had to have a good show of support from key trading partners. BAe were responsive and played a pivotal role in helping to put together a package. The idea was for BAe, London City Airport and Virgin to loan Cityjet stg£250,000 each, together with a moratorium on payment for services up to stg£500,000 in each case. This debt would carry an interest charge but no repayments were due for two years. A condition of this support was that the three institutional investors in Cityjet would inject additional share capital of stg£350,000 between them. The total value of the support amounted to stg£2.5 million in cash flow benefit and was deemed sufficient to sustain the cash position of the airline.

This was vital breathing space but we were still going to be dependent on a considerable uplift in revenue to keep us flying straight. On the promotions front, we continued with our aggressive marketing but I was growing weary of the quality of output we were getting from our advertising agency with the notable exception of their highly creative senior copywriter.

I met Tom Power initially through an imaginative promotional opportunity where we sponsored a 72-footer he was chartering with his fellow captain, Colm Barrington, in the Round Ireland Yacht Race being held in that June of 1994. We paid no money but gave the guys tickets to London City with a face value of £20,000. They in turn sold these at face value to their business contacts. The funding for the race was secured, we filled empty seats with businesspeople who would hopefully fly with us again and the publicity we got from "Virgin Cityjet" being covered as the race leader for four days was worth a lot.

We put together a practical alternative to using an advertising agency. We assembled the components of design, copywriting and media buying and did it ourselves more effectively and for less cost, forming a marketing kitchen cabinet with Tom as the catalyst among a small band of freelance specialists in scripting and production of radio ads. Mark Quinn brought his unique creativity in design to the party. The unmistakable unique personality of Cityjet would be stamped on everything we would do from then on. This would subsequently prove to be a formula that could carry our message further, build true affinity with our audience and be retained in the consciousness of our target market for far less cost than before. It required huge commitment from me, the CEO, as the public face of the airline but it was fun and very successful. This was impact marketing at its most effective. It would prove to be our lifeline with the public, creditors, shareholders and regulators. We came across as we were: straight-up, no bullshit, no excuses and promises you could count on; a human airline.

Through all this time, our constant ally in the Virgin camp was Hugh Welburn, who really believed in our strategic objectives. He never tired in lending his considerable acumen to planning schedules and fares with an eye to exploiting weaknesses in our competitors' offers. It was Hugh who wholly endorsed the "Book of Ten" concept, which was a revolutionary development at the time — buy a book of ten return tickets in executive class for a fifteen per cent discount. Fully flexible, the tickets could be used in any name and, subject to twenty-four hours notice of intent to travel, a guaranteed seat irrespective of the booked load. "The Book" became a bestseller and was ultimately copied by Aer Lingus some eighteen months later.

But the storm clouds were still gathering. The mood with the managers we had to deal with in Virgin was very off. The "anti" bias was still strong and thinly concealed. Even Syd Pennington, in his role as managing director, was beginning to take a tougher line with us in the presence of others. I believe he was coming under increasing pressure from a select bunch of his reporting managers, who seemed to be having some success in undermining his executive authority in relation to the support he had been showing for Cityjet. I personally had the strong suspicion that these guys were possibly working at eroding Branson's confidence in Syd. I had felt Syd's appointment to the MD role had not been entirely popular within the management of the airline. Here was a highly skilled and professional commercial manager who saw things pretty straight and he called them accordingly. Bullshit didn't survive long in front of Syd. Sadly, Syd left Virgin some months later. I believe he saw it then and hopefully still sees it now as a better career move.

They gave us advance notice. We were being summoned to what they billed as a make-or-break meeting on 21 July. We read it for what it was: a summary execution. I believed they had managed to persuade Branson to stay out of the meeting, as there could be no chance of a reprieve for the little Irish airline that they felt he had become too attached to. We prepared carefully. There was no point in going into this latest battle without a tactical device of devastating power. We decided to bring with us our lawyer, Siobhan Lohan of Ireland's largest legal firm, A&L Goodbody. Siobhan had been a friend for years. Aviation law, airlines and leasing contracts were her particular areas of competence. But Siobhan was also a very fine commercial lawyer with a good nose for how to fight hard.

Once again we also prevailed on Robin Southwell of BAe to come with us. He had done more than anyone to put the very recent rescue funding package in place and here, less than a month later, Virgin were posturing to potentially take action that would effectively wipe out the airline and leave no realistic way of debt recovery for the providers of the financial lifeline, including Virgin themselves.

The meeting commenced and we were treated to a long diatribe from the Virgin Finance Director as to all of the very good reasons, in his opinion, why the franchise agreement should be terminated forthwith by Virgin, who would be acting absolutely within their contractual rights. We listened and listened. And now it was approaching that time when the fuse on our tactical device needed to be lit.

"You're insolvent and therefore in breach of the franchise agreement," declared the Finance Director. Siobhan spoke quietly. "Would you care to define insolvency?" she invited. "But perhaps I should advise you that unless you are familiar with the definition under Irish law, anything else you say is irrelevant, as we are talking about an Irish company." The key difference, of course, was that under Irish law a company is only insolvent if the directors believe they cannot meet their debts to creditors as they fall due. In our case, we had kept our principal creditors (including Virgin, BAe and Mowlems, the owners of LCY, who had supported the recent cash call) fully informed and had re-scheduled repayments with their permission.

But what came next can only be described as a show-stopping delivery. Siobhan went on to say that we had listened to the Virgin team outline their view of the hopelessness of the Cityjet financial circumstances. However, she pointed out that it was her view that Virgin could be construed to have been responsible in part for much of what had gone wrong in terms of failing to produce revenue to target in the UK, in spite of their spending all of Cityjet's London marketing budget of stg£450,000 in just six weeks. Virgin's insistence on the implementation of an early morning flight out of London, which produced huge operational losses, and Virgin's refusal to allow Cityjet to reduce catering costs were further examples of how they had imposed themselves in the management of Cityjet. For all of these, but more significantly by delaying the transfer of Cityjet's rightful cash from ticket sales, Virgin had cast themselves in the role of acting as "shadow directors" of the company. Siobhan carried on by explaining that, under Irish law, any person or persons found to have so acted as a "shadow director" of a company that subsequently fails can be held liable for the financial consequences. We had their attention. In fact, they were so shaken that we knew the bomb had landed. I don't know how many lives we had used up at this stage, but this cat's tail wasn't hanging between his legs as we defiantly marched out of the room and headed for home. For now, we were untouchable. We had bought a few more valuable weeks.

Operations were demanding. The BAe 146 was proving to be a difficult aircraft to keep serviceable. We were beset by engine issues and wiring problems. When we had a technical snag we went into overdrive to minimise the fallout with passengers who had become regular users of our service. In targeting the regular traveller with business in the City, we were pitching into a very close-knit community where word among them is passed quickly. That was both good and bad. Great to get more people to try us but a disaster if we upset people with a long delay. We were, by our own doing, highly visible and accessible. It was this accessibility, especially for passengers with a grievance, that helped build our early reputation of actually giving a damn about what customer service means. We accepted the inevitability of breakdowns and resolved to turn every one of them into an opportunity for building a better relationship with our customers. This helped enormously to instil a sense of loyalty in our regular passengers. It made them less likely to spread bad stories about delays and more likely to talk about how we took the chaos out of a crisis and managed their concerns.

There were many messy situations caused by technical problems with aircraft in the early months. One which I vividly recall serves to give a sense of how we felt for our passengers when things went wrong. Our last flight out of London City in the evening was what we called our sweeper flight at 8.30 pm. On Fridays, this was as full as our two earlier evening departures from the City. There was a curfew on the City Airport of 9.00, in compliance with local environment regulations. The one flight we just didn't need to have a technical snag on was one with a half-hour of fixing time before the shutters came down and we would be locked in with our passengers. On this particular Friday, we were up against it. We negotiated a discretion of an extra hour on the curfew to give more time to remedy the situation but it turned out that we would need to change a component which, of course, was sitting in our stores in Dublin. It was too late to fly it over and make it in before lights out and also now too late to bus our passengers to Stansted or Heathrow to fly home with the competition. Along with the management team, I was in the flight operations room, watching this customer service horror story worsen by the half-hour. We hired a bus and took our utterly frustrated passengers to a hotel where we gave them dinner, drinks and a complimentary phone call.

The next morning, Saturday, I was standing on the ramp at Dublin Airport to greet our overnight passengers as they picked their way down the steps. I owned up as the guy they could direct their irritation and anger at. I felt awful for them, but I knew it was important not to hide from this and also to show the staff that I could empathise with them having to represent Cityjet in similar scenarios, of which inevitably there would be a few. But just like when you fall off a horse or a bike, the essential thing is to get back up again as soon as possible. That's why I handed everybody a free ticket to get them to come back to us quickly and hopefully bury the memory of a bad experience.

It was all too blatantly clear to me that Virgin were not good commercial partner material for us. They were fantastic in the domain of front-line customer service and the quality of our cabin crew and in-flight service bore testimony to that. But there it stopped. Their sales capability on short-haul activities was abysmal. Their understanding of short-haul routes and how they have to be marketed was considerably less than ours, and we were brand new to this business. Notwithstanding the fact that it formed no part of our agreement, it was remarkable that there was not even an informal expression of interest in the technical workings of our flight operations or engineering.

I was rapidly beginning to realise that Virgin, in respect of regional airline operations and the management of a commercial partnership with a smaller player, were just as inexperienced as their name suggested. But much worse than that was the constant confrontational aspect of our interaction with these people. I speculated to myself that on the basis that Branson didn't pay his staff well, this was, with a few notable exceptions, manifest in the calibre of managers we were forced to deal with. The chief method employed by Virgin in the management of the relationship with Cityjet was constant referral to what was in the franchise agreement and how Cityjet was not in compliance with some clause or other. The thing that really stuck in my mind about this whole unhappy dreadful relationship was the fact that Virgin, who enjoyed an image of taking on the establishment and striking a blow for the little guy, was demonstrating itself to be an institutional bully. Their lack of enterprising flair was remarkable; not on any single occasion, with the absolute exception of Hugh Welburn and Syd Pennington, did anyone in Virgin ever come up with even a hint of a pragmatic initiative as to how they might help Cityjet make progress in growing its way out of trouble.

I knew that, apart from more investment capital, we were in dire need of a partnership with an airline that understood the day-to-day challenges of operating a regional scheduled service. BAe introduced us to an American investment intermediary who had strong relationships with the principals in Air Wisconsin, a regional airline flying feeder flights on contract to United. Air Wisconsin were the last remaining US regional airline who had managed to find a way of viably operating the BAe 146 against the background of the very restrictive pilots' scope clause agreement. Air Wisconsin had their own arrangement with their pilots which facilitated the striking of a deal with United to fly in their colours and provide them with feeder traffic to their hubs. Luke and I hopped on a Virgin evening flight to JFK to meet up with our contact man the next morning and be introduced to the main shareholder in Air Wisconsin, Richard Bartlett.

Chapter Seven

GETTING USED TO LIVING ON FUMES

It was mid-August and Manhattan was steaming. To be techni-cally correct, Richard Bartlett's firm managed a number of high-value investment trusts on behalf of some of New York's "old money". The office was impressive and he even more so. He was an intelligent, incisive investor who displayed a great grasp of the airline he was already invested in. We strutted our stuff and told him the story of how we got Cityjet in the air and levelled with him about how difficult it was to keep it there. He was genuinely in-trigued as to how we, with no airline experience whatsoever, had managed to persuade Branson to grant us a franchise. We told him we were envious of the Air Wisconsin model because it represented a very low-risk proposition, with United Airlines buying the seats on all routes. This was the kind of franchise we desperately needed but could see no way of getting at that point in time. Richard Bart-lett was gripped by our enthusiasm and determination to make a success of what we had started. He openly proclaimed that he had ambition to invest in an airline operation in Europe to leverage what they had learned from their investment in Air Wisconsin.

There would be more meetings and endless transatlantic phone calls between Richard and myself. The dialogue would continue over a very protracted period and would turn out to be one of a number of such drawn-out exploratory relationships with other more established regional airlines in pursuit of a suitable trade partner/investor.

BAe became even more interested in our ever-increasingly dubious credit risk. They had been patient and understanding of our difficulties and had seen first-hand that the Virgin relationship brought with it more challenges than the initially anticipated benefits. As October progressed, so too did the anxiety levels of our "partners". I was on a transfer bus from Gatwick to Heathrow, having spent a difficult morning with Virgin in their Crawley offices. The call to my mobile gave me an incredibly fortunate piece of news. Back home, the Airline Transport Users Association (affiliated to the Chambers of Commerce in Ireland), who conduct an annual poll of the top 1,000 business executives to determine their views on airlines and airports, had declared Cityjet not only the winner of the Best Airline on the Dublin to London Route, but also the Airline of the Year ahead of all other airlines operating into and out of Ireland.

This was PR gold dust from a marketing perspective; but more significantly, it was incalculably important to us in staying the hand of key trading partners who might be harbouring certain "pull the plug" type thoughts. The awards ceremony was set for the Burlington Hotel in Dublin for lunchtime. That same morning, BAe's top team, led by Robin Southwell, arrived in Dublin to talk turkey: Cityjet would have to quicken the pace of additional investor support in order to pay its way on aircraft leases and other vital support services. I had little choice but to tell them that our meeting was going to be interrupted by the not-so-insignificant matter of my having to go to collect our award for Airline of the Year. Of course, I brought them along to witness firsthand that obviously we were doing something right. With only ten months of operations behind, us we had scooped the prize ahead of Aer Lingus, British Midland, British Airways and Ryanair. The target market we had gone after were saying clearly that we had hit the spot. I also invited some people from Virgin management so that the full impact of this enormously encouraging endorsement from the business community could be felt in Crawley.

So there I was, feeling a bit like a prisoner out on parole without the handcuffs. My potential jailors in the form of BAe and Virgin listened as I belted out the Cityjet "success story" to the travel trade and the press. There would be a party night for the staff to celebrate this milestone achievement and Branson was coming to town for that, plus another publicity drive through the media. But celebratory thoughts in my head would have little time to take root. No sooner had the last click of a press camera finished than it was into a meeting room in the hotel to receive what was written on the tablets brought by BAe.

Robin Southwell was clear in his mind that the airline should be supported but it should not fall exclusively on BAe. He was advocating that the axis of vested interests — namely Virgin, Mowlems and themselves — should collectively continue to apply their minds and financial resources to get Cityjet through its growing pains phase. He believed that Branson and Mowlems plc, who built and owned City Airport, should lend their respective shoulders to the wheel alongside BAe. With such a united approach to support, it should prove more palatable for the existing shareholders to inject more capital. So we embarked on this course of action over the next few months, a heavy programme of successive meetings being held with all parties represented in an effort to construct a support package for Cityjet.

In parallel with this were a number of other potential roads to travel in the search for capital and potential pragmatic alliances with other operators. BAe introduced us to another of their customers in the form of National Jet Systems (NJS) of Australia. NJS operated a fleet of more than twenty 146s on contract to Qantas on their domestic route network. Owned by Adele Lloyd and Warren Seymour, who was also CEO of the airline, NJS had developed a highly successful airline and had made sense out of the BAe 146 and its notorious technical and financial challenges.

They came to us for a few days and undertook a very high-level due diligence of where we were at. They were interested but not in a hurry to invest. There would be a few more exchanges with them in succeeding months, but it would be another four years before Warren and Adele would return for one of the most bizarre chapters in this story. But that will have to wait for now.

The management of London City Airport and their owners Mowlems were also on the lookout for potential investors for Cityjet. They had been approached by a potential buyer for the airport, whom they introduced to us. This potential investor had succeeded in captivating the interest of Mowlems, a major plc, and proceeded to progress his "bid" over the following few months. The general thrust of where this was going was that the aspiring new owner of the airport would also have a substantial holding in an established 146 operator. In this way, approaches could be made to large airlines which would not ordinarily operate the BAe 146 with a view to getting them to develop routes out of London City. They could wet-lease Cityjet and so avoid the mega investment expense of having to gear up for operations with another aircraft type while still only in the proving stages of route viability. (A wet lease is where another operator's aircraft is hired in together with their flight deck and cabin crew and the flights are conducted under their operators' certificate but flown under our flight designator numbers.) Sound thinking, and it could have worked . . . but for one thing. The man ultimately turned out to be a con artist.

Admittedly, this guy had a lot of people fooled, including us. Eventually I gave in to my suspicions and hired a leading detective agency in London to check out his background. He had hidden his trail well, but not well enough, because we eventually discovered that he had other identities. He also had form, the sort of form that would not exactly qualify him as a reputable character with whom you could do business. We shared our information with Mowlems and saved them and ourselves a lot of time and hassle with a waster. Within months we would find them a real buyer for the airport, someone who would close the deal.

The finer details of a potential support package, which became known as "The Workout Plan", from the interested parties finally began to emerge in January 1995 and the succeeding weeks saw an intense effort to get everybody to buy into it. By now BAe were owed a lot of money in terms of deferred lease payments, maintenance reserves and a loan they had advanced to Cityjet. London City Airport were owed £0.8 million if they were going strictly by their published tariff of charges. Both of these companies were prepared to restructure and very importantly reduce debt in exchange for a return to regular payments for services as they fell due together, with long-term commitments from Cityjet to higher charges and extended contracts. Virgin were being asked to do the same but they were seeking to impose unacceptable terms in the form of a deferred convertible into equity "at a rate unfavourable to Cityjet" as their Finance Director proposed. BAe and Mowlems were up for it but Virgin dragged their feet. It was getting harder to breathe in this thinner air but we were still alive and could continue to look for more oxygen out there.

NJS came back briefly on the scene. They indicated that the price of their investment support would be for us to deliver Aer Lingus into the equation as a customer on behalf of whom we could operate flights. This would replicate the successful model NJS enjoyed with Qantas. Sure, easy enough to arrange — with the competitor who would rather see us die. Air Wisconsin were still circling in the distance and were making noises about their continued potential interest. I kept the relationship with Crossair in an attempt to exploit any promising opportunity for us.

Around this time, we also had commenced a relationship with Apax Partners, the investment house in London. They took us seriously and expended a considerable amount of time and effort in doing due diligence and constructing an investment prospectus to take to their private clients. One of these was a very interesting man from Brussels called Felix Grovett. I met him a few times and he was certainly giving me the vibes that our ambition to develop more routes from European cities into London City resonated strongly with him. Again, as with so many other "perfect fits", it evaporated within two or three months of the initial engagement.

Richard Branson himself did offer to take over Cityjet in a phone call to me on St Patrick's Day. The only problem was the price. He felt £1 should secure the company and "You could tell your shareholders that I'll take care of all the outstanding issues with creditors". It was probably exactly the kick in the arse I needed. I scarcely recall a moment of higher motivation to see off any predatory action from any quarter in our perilous state of acute vulnerability. I resolved to get stronger in my efforts to keep things going, to find money and the right kind of partner.

We were also in talks with other parties such as ING, Baronsmead (who had invested in Gill Air), Maersk Airlines, Northern and Shell and a number of high net worth private investors, both in the UK and Ireland. These kind of exploratory discussions take a long time and rarely lead anywhere but you have to keep trying.

Our other very pressing and ever-present objective was to examine how we could practically increase our flying activity to boost revenues. We had constantly been evaluating new routes over the past number of months. The one that kept re-appearing on our radar was Dublin to Brussels. It was a business route with Irish civil servants travelling always in business class, accounting for a substantial portion of the very high revenues available. We worked out a schedule that would allow us to serve our existing commitment to Dublin/London City and still operate a twice-daily service to and from Brussels without any increase in fleet size or crew complement. We had a difficult battle with Virgin who felt this would over-stretch us but they accepted that we must try to expand our revenue base. Our competition would be Aer Lingus who operated twice a day in a code share with Sabena. What we didn't know was that Club Travel, a prominent travel agent in Dublin, had done an extraordinary deal with Sabena and was about to corner the Irish civil servants' business on the route.

We launched on 1 July and the then Taoiseach, John Bruton, officiated at the sending-off of the first flight from Dublin. Our advertising was to the point and clearly aimed at this public sector traffic. Our sales team were energetic and focused on the buyers of travel in all Government departments. It didn't take long to find out why we were not getting what we expected to be our market share of the front of the plane high revenue. Club Travel had been awarded a special contract by a number of Government departments whereby they were the provider of seats and hotel accommodation to Brussels. The twist however was that the seats, all on Aer Lingus flights, were supplied to Club Travel by Sabena, not Aer Lingus. We dug and we found out more. Sabena were paying Club a staggering twenty-three per cent commission on sales. Sabena were buying the seats from Aer Lingus at the rate of £108 per return trip. At the time, the Aer Lingus price for a business class ticket to Brussels was £600. Club would heavily discount the fare to the government, using some of their fat commission to do so. The civil servants would still travel on Aer Lingus flights, collect their Aer Lingus TAB frequent flyer points and everybody was happy. The Government wasn't seen to be favouring the national carrier at a time when it was debarred from any state funding by the EU Commission. Meanwhile, Aer Lingus flights were full to Brussels and Cityjet was frozen out of the market.

We brought in our lawyers, A&L Goodbody, whose EU competition law competence was excellent. I went to see the Department of Enterprise and Employment, who confirmed the deal with Club Travel. No, there had been no advertising of a competition for the placing of air travel for civil servants to Brussels. I wrote to every Government minister to determine their policy and practice in relation to the selection of airlines in respect of civil servants on official business to Brussels and London. The responses were startling in terms of their straightforward confirmation of an unambiguous support for the national carrier in almost all cases. Unwittingly, this simple letter of enquiry I had penned had resulted in the compilation of an incontrovertible book of evidence against the Irish Government in the matter of a flagrant breach of the EU Public Procurement Directive. No competition was held and an exclusive contract had been awarded in relation to the Dublin/Brussels route in respect of public servants' travel. We had now also enough evidence to suggest that a directive to civil servants was in place in most Government departments to travel exclusively on Aer Lingus flights and that of course meant Cityjet was being discriminated against on our core route to London as well.

We had two issues to tackle. The first was with the EU Commission and what action we could encourage them to take against the Irish Government for their breach of the Public Procurement Directive; the second was the matter of indirect state aid being routed to Aer Lingus contrary to the strict EU embargo on all such aid.

My education on how to navigate the corridors of the EU Commission and their famed DG7 and DG4 divisions was about to commence and would progress rapidly over the next three months. But it was important to rattle Aer Lingus's cage, as we were losing blood at a savage pace on the new route. I phoned Gary McGann, the recently appointed CEO of Aer Lingus. At the ensuing meeting in their head office, just five days after we had launched our Brussels service, I very clearly outlined the issue we had with what we interpreted as a cosy arrangement. The EU Commission had sanctioned the granting of state aid in the form of a £175 million equity injection by the Irish government, the sole shareholder in Aer Lingus. We told Aer Lingus that we interpreted the support of the Irish government in terms of its employees availing of the Club Travel/Sabena purchase of seats on Aer Lingus flights to Brussels as additional state aid over and above the £175 million sanctioned by the EU. Furthermore, we were confident that this "exclusive" arrangement of seats being sold by Club Travel to Irish government departments was in clear breach of the EU public procurement directive as no competition had been held for the placement of this business.

The response from the other side of the table was calm and co-gently put. They were confident they were not in breach of the state aid rules imposed by the EU Commission and that it would be difficult for Cityjet to make any of this stick. Pearse and myself were completely taken by surprise with what came next. Here were the senior executives telling us they were impressed with our progress on Dublin/London City and that we had carved out a niche with the business community through the provision of a highly professional quality service. They went on to suggest that it would be much more productive for all concerned to explore how the two airlines might work together in the future instead of bickering over the travel habits of civil servants. These were tough times for Aer Lingus who had come close to going under financially and quite possibly would have done had it not been for the investment of £175 million. The consequence of this permitted last slug of state aid was a very careful monitoring of expansion during the three years immediately after the investment. There would therefore be a requirement for discretion, but they would like to commence exploratory talks with Cityjet to arrive at a mutual assessment on the feasibility of the two airlines working together. We agreed that I was to prepare a position paper covering the main issues to be examined at the first meeting to be held later in the month.

Our first meeting took place in the Shelbourne Hotel two weeks later. The dialogue on my position paper was open and frank and there was little doubting that the intent of the Aer Lingus executives was to find a way of forming a partnership with Cityjet. This would more than likely involve them taking a minority equity stake in us. Their idea was to market the Cityjet brand as having a service partnership with Aer Lingus and utilising the national carrier's distribution system. This was real "wake up and pinch me, I must be dreaming" stuff. But it was happening and the timing from our perspective was fantastic. We committed to a series of meetings over the next few weeks as we all agreed that we needed to get to a decision point soon.

The next meeting was almost three weeks later in the Conrad Hotel. Intense and detailed, we concentrated on the question of investment, future development of Cityjet and branding issues. We examined the potential pricing mechanism on investment by Aer Lingus in Cityjet, the timing of the deal, the fees structure for goods and services to be provided by Aer Lingus. The pace over that month of August 1995 was frenetic. We continued to meet in neutral venues. We had in-depth discussion on the strategic intent of entering into an agreement and we specifically drove towards reaching a consensus view on marketing, branding and distribution. We finally got to produce a draft of the Heads of Terms which reflected the agreed position of the parties on all issues, including setting the end of November as the preferred commencement date of the new relationship. We resolved to commence work on the detailed business and implementation plan the following week.

However, a problem surfaced. I got a call from Aer Lingus to say there had been a leak. Their story was that they had been obliged to show the draft Heads of Terms to their lawyers, who were emphatic in their advice not to enter into formal investment discussions ahead of 31 December. The significance of this date was the scheduled time for the injection of the last remaining £50 million state aid injection for Aer Lingus.

As a precaution, it was suggested that a fresh Heads of Terms be produced with coded references inserted to protect the true identities of the parties in the interim. I was assured that "this is not the old Aer Lingus messing you around" and that we could anticipate the draft outline agreement being signed off by the end of the month. There now was a clear shared understanding at that point of exactly what could be executed between the parties, given due cognisance of the fears of Aer Lingus in relation to the state aid. It was also understood that both parties would proceed to incorporate the respective real identities into an agreed document without fear of consequence once the end of December had passed.

Meanwhile, work was supposed to continue on the business plan. But it didn't. Progress from the Aer Lingus side was not being made. I wrote a note to record my deep sense of frustration at the lack of momentum. We met. In a show of good faith, a commitment was made to work on a code share or seat purchase arrangement on Dublin/London City, the sub-contracting of the Aer Lingus Dublin/Milan service and the provision of reservations services as an alternative to the Virgin system.

Throughout the period we had been engaging with Aer Lingus, we were continuing to be hammered on Dublin/Brussels. We were getting virtually none of the lucrative Government traffic. Our representations to the EU Commission yielded the clearest indication that the Irish Government, Sabena and Aer Lingus were all involved in a blatant attempt to distort competition and we were being encouraged strongly by our legal advisers to take action. Our contention was that Sabena were acting as a phantom operator on the route as they bought all of their seats from Aer Lingus at a steep discount and then marketed them on through Club Travel to the highly prized Government sector. By manipulation of the retail price, made possible by the exceedingly generous commission of twenty-three per cent from Sabena, Club Travel were undercutting the Aer Lingus published business class fares by a huge margin. By not competing on price, Aer Lingus were in effect facilitating the sale of Sabena tickets to civil servants on Aer Lingus flights. The civil servants still got their Aer Lingus tab points and the Aer Lingus service they were comfortable with — and everybody wins except Cityjet. It all seemed too cosy an arrangement, with the devastating power of keeping the newcomer, Cityjet, out of the game.

Not for the first time was I in the middle of a "Catch 22" scenario. If Aer Lingus were really genuine in their efforts to form a partnership with us, then it wouldn't be the brightest thing to kick them in the balls with a legal action over their role in the Brussels strangulation. On the other hand, if they were deliberately leading us on to distract us as we bled ever more on a daily basis, then I really was a fool.

I went for a calculated punch. I wrote to Aer Lingus to request formally that they discontinue their block space agreement with Sabena. At a subsequent meeting, they advised us that they were making efforts to persuade Sabena to curb the activities of Club Travel in relation to the aggressive pricing of seats to Irish government departments. To take the sting out of the mood building between us, Aer Lingus agreed at the same meeting that if Cityjet were to operate a Dublin/Milan service via Brussels, they would purchase a significant number of seats at a reasonably attractive price.

Just over a week later, Aer Lingus called us to say they were sorry but they had made a mistake in their calculations and the price they could pay for those Milan seats was now a lot lower. From our perspective, it would mean operating at a huge loss. Still no deal. We reworked the plan and decided the Milan service could be run via London City with an improved commitment from Aer Lingus to buy seats on the Cityjet Dublin/Brussels service. All that was needed was a sign of tacit support from a number of senior members of their Board. That, however, couldn't be delivered at this time, I was told. Better to revisit everything in January when the dust had settled on the final state aid payment, or words to that effect. After four solid months of intense negotiating, planning and hoping, we were as empty-handed as when we had started the dialogue, plus we were in deeper trouble with the poor results on Dublin/Brussels.

I couldn't let things just sit like that. It was worth another go and so I arranged another high level meeting. We covered a lot of ground, culminating with an agreement in principle that, effective from the following February (1996), we would co-brand. Aer Lingus would give Cityjet reservations and distribution support and a route development programme would be implemented. This would most probably include London City/Milan, London City/Barcelona, London City/Brussels and with London City/Nice and Dublin/Paris Orly a possibility. On the big issue of equity participation, they suggested this should not take place too quickly after the last slug of state aid but that firm equity options in Cityjet could be granted to Aer Lingus with penalty pricing for delaying the timing of a conversion. To give effect to this complex package, Board approval would of course be required and that would not be possible ahead of the end of the year and the final injection of state aid. "Well, what about a letter of intent?" I asked. They undertook to prepare an internal briefing paper over the next two days, consult informally with a select number of Board directors and, if they were supportive, a "qualified" letter of intent that would seek formal board approval on 1 February might be possible.

I never got a letter of intent, "qualified" or otherwise. But there would be a lot more to come in the never boring and extraordinary relationship with Aer Lingus.

Chapter Eight

LIKE LIVE TV, YOU CAN'T MESS UP

Who was running the airline while all this was going on? As always, we continued to juggle and manage the very many balls we had in the air and the numerous plates we had spinning on sticks. Teamwork had been redefined by Cityjet and the commitment of people was quite remarkable. From the start, we had set out to give a level of customer care that was exceptional. How our passengers viewed us was the barometer for measuring our performance. It governed everything we did. It influenced how we anticipated problems. An unscheduled breakdown of an aircraft was a commercially life-threatening event and we applied maximum resources to remedying quickly. With two aircraft we had no back-up cover. Our ability to recover quickly had to be brilliant, not just all right. The weeks were long, with the mobile phone pretty much a permanent attachment to the ear over every weekend. There was lots of very heroic stuff going on around flight operations, putting in place initiatives to retrieve messy upsets caused by technical and weather disruptions. London City Airport had its bad days when we simply could not land there due to its CAT 1 status (the categories are determined by the type of landing aid equipment installed at the particular airport and the equipment onboard the aircraft); other London airports boasted CAT 2B capability. Put simply, if the visibility was on the deck, we couldn't get in there. Whereas the historic weather patterns suggested the prospect of no more than two or three such days in November, with another one or two in

February, that autumn season of 1995 was hard going with fog featuring too often. Christmas week that year was very difficult at all London airports, with persistent snow causing major disruption. When it got really bad for us at City, we transferred some of our flights to Southend to benefit from the thawing effect of the coastal salt air, which proved to be the difference in getting our heavily booked loads of passengers home on time.

When you switch on an airline, it just has to be kept going. You can't just stop when trouble happens. It is a very public, highly visible business where you have to perform every flight every day for a real live audience — your passengers. The pressure is unrelenting; it is truly a business that never sleeps and consequently those responsible for it don't get much of that either. Awaiting the arrival of an aircraft from Brussels at five in the evening was nerve-wracking. We needed the plane to refuel, re-cater and head to London to lift a heavy evening load home from the City. An ATC slot delay could wreck your head. But we had a balanced amount of stress in our operational day. Any given early morning, I would hold my breath as I waited for operations to answer me as I drove to the office. Was the 7.15 on time to City? Any delay on the second launch to London? Every morning we were dependent on the early morning arrival from Brussels not being delayed, as this was also our second morning flight to London. One of our big appeals to the business market were these two early morning flights, less than an hour apart — a credible alternative to the gaggle of flights to Heathrow in the same time band.

Then there was the dreaded news we never wanted to get about something major, like having to do an engine change; if misfortune had to strike, please let it be at night when we had some time to sort it. This was amputation in another guise. Fourteen hours of downtime to swap a dead engine for a raw one out of a box, according to the book. We got very good at it; we had plenty of practice. Later when we were even more experienced and when we could afford to have "dressed" engines in waiting (i.e. ones with the accessory plumbing such as fuel pumps and generators fitted on top) we would achieve engine changes in under eight hours. Of course, the 146, being four-engined, had a different set-up in terms of the "dressed" kit, depending on whether the engine was being slung in an "inner" or an "outer" position on-wing. If we could have afforded it and had there been an ample supply of spare engines around at that early stage of our operations, we would have had two spare engines on standby, one in "inner" dress mode and the second as an "outer". This would take our engine change time down to five hours. But cash didn't stretch to afford us such luxury in those days and we had to make do with an engine in "neutral" dress mode, which meant no change out of eight hours. We kept our cool, we stuck at it and we learned.

The heavy dating of Aer Lingus through the late summer and autumn was not our exclusive line of pursuit to get married to an airline partner and relieve our calamitous financial position. I had a really serious go at persuading Virgin to get off the fence, stop standing on our oxygen pipe of revenue every month and become an equity partner. In September, I went to see Frances Farrow, one of the rising stars in Virgin, whom I regarded as a moderate in the political scheme of things in Crawley, with plenty of common sense. Notwithstanding her earlier role in cautioning Branson not to announce the new Virgin/Cityjet deal on live TV when we were in the throes of getting the franchise agreement sorted, I had since come to regard her as a pragmatist. She had recently been elevated from being the in-house legal counsel to an executive director position and Branson valued her opinions. I laid out very clearly that the franchise agreement didn't work in terms of cost to our P&L given the level of available fares on our routes. I reasoned that if Virgin were to become a shareholder in Cityjet, I was very confident of securing substantial institutional investment support to expand the capital base and catapult the airline into a position of critical mass. We were agreed on the need to scale Cityjet. To my surprise, we were also saying the same thing about how the Virgin Atlantic brand was wrong for Cityjet and that it should have been marketed under the name of Virgin Cityjet, which is what both Branson and myself had wanted from the start. There was also unanimity between us in the belief that the people in Virgin's marketing department had hijacked the show and exceeded their position of influence under the convenient cover of "brand protection".

Frances admitted that Virgin had very badly handled the relationship with Cityjet but my "to the point" faxes and letters had unhinged many of Virgin's senior executives. She went on to say that there was now a growing belief in Virgin that I was getting ready to pull away from Virgin, having "coat-tailed" the launch of the Cityjet brand on the back of Virgin. Overall, however, she felt strongly that Branson would support the endorsement of a Virgin Cityjet brand but in terms of equity participation he was only comfortable with one hundred per cent or nothing. Having seen up close what working for Branson was most probably like, a total takeover wasn't very appealing.

With little or no early prospect of fresh investment capital, we focused on raising bank support secured against our forward revenues. Luke and I went back to Woodchester, where we were both well known given that our former respective companies had been bought by them. We negotiated a complex arrangement which would see Woodchester advance Cityjet money secured on the sold tickets, revenue from which would flow through to us some weeks later. The problem was that Virgin were still acting as the holder of our purse and it required them to give a formal undertaking to the Bank to pass on the money. With the past form of some in Virgin, in their attitude towards Cityjet, this was not going to be easy. It took a few weeks and a lot of scrutiny and more meetings with lawyers but we got there. Yet another lifeline was thrown to us in the form of the secured bank facility.

One of the repeated potential private investors we kept calling on in Dublin was Dermot Desmond. He had recently come through some tough business times and was just emerging triumphant and extremely wealthy. To be fair, he was consistent through every meeting. He was not attracted to the notion of becoming an airline shareholder but he was supportive in spirit for what we were trying to do.

As we were getting ready to take our leave from Dermot Desmond's office in Ferry House, I turned to him and said, "Well, if you won't invest in Cityjet, how about becoming our new landlords in London City?" He was instantly captivated. Luke and I quickly outlined how desperate Mowlems were to off-load the airport. They had incurred a liability of stg£84 million to date in terms of construction and operational losses. As a primary contractor in Canary Wharf and with demand for the abundant space now built there at a complete stop, they were hurting and needed to fly to cash quickly.

By this stage our ongoing talks with Mowlems about reducing the enormous rates of charge for our Dublin service from the international to the UK domestic rate were yielding little. The differential in pricing between International and UK domestic designated flights was 2:1 and our fares to Dublin were no more than others were getting for London City to Edinburgh.

From our involvement in the talks with the "outed" impostor purporting to be a serous purchaser, we knew the asking price for the airport was just under stg£30 million. We arranged for Dermot Desmond to meet with John Marshall, the Managing Director of Mowlems, within the following two weeks. The deal-making moved fast. On a Saturday morning, as I was watching a boys' soccer match in a local park, my mobile buzzed. For a change, it wasn't Cityjet flight ops, but Michael Walsh, who was involved in all of Dermot's deals. Michael wanted my view, in a hurry, on what I thought would be the lowest clinching price. I called it at stg£24.5 million, half a million more than they eventually would pay. Not bad for an asset that would be valued at more than twelve times that figure some nine years later. Before year-end, there was a new owner of London City Airport. We hadn't succeeded in getting him as an investor in the airline, but he was now assuming the role of one of our major creditors. And we could talk to him. I felt it had to be positive. I hoped he would be supportive going forward.

Among the other people I was talking to about potential investment partners was a man called Peter Grut who had an "in" with the family who owned Malmo Aviation. Malmo were interesting for a number of reasons. They operated a fleet of BAe 146s on domestic routes in Sweden but they also were the first operator to fly a relatively long sector into London City from Stockholm. We had "borrowed" their standard operating procedures (SOPs) through Captain Chris Nielsen, who transferred to us from Malmo during our licence application phase. It would be a year later before the relationship with Malmo would take off in dramatic circumstances. But for now, that was a lifetime away given what we were destined to go through over the intervening months.

The drive for more ticket sales was unrelenting. We pushed hard with the travel agents specialising in business travel and we spent a lot of time going direct to the companies with regular business in London City and Brussels. Our marketing was innovatively effective. The combined internal/external team was working well and we succeeded in maintaining a constant presence in the eyes of our target market without spending a lot of money, which of course we didn't have. The invitations kept coming in to speak at all sorts of events and I never refused. I knew it was important to keep building the profile of the airline as I wanted to create an aura of it being unstoppable. This was as important for the staff to see as it was for the flying public. When it came down to it, the support of the regular business flyers was a crucial component of our survival during our yet-to-come most difficult moments.

I was introduced to Gay Byrne by Mary Purcell, our sales manager, at a wedding. His *Late Late Show* had featured in a most fragile time of the final days of pre-birth for Cityjet. I had been aware of his very keen affinity with aviation and he seemed genuinely interested in how we were doing. I followed up by contacting his researcher for the show and worked hard at pitching the human interest side of the story behind the airline. I was eventually lined up for a live interview on the *Late Late* in a few weeks' time in January.

Heading into that Christmas of 1995, I was only certain of one thing. We had survived our second year of operations. Our chances of making it had gone up in spite of everything. I didn't know if Aer Lingus were jerking us around or if they had an honourable intent to do meaningful business with us. There was a new owner of London City Airport, with whom we were well acquainted, and we had been responsible for planting the seed in his head to go and buy it. Three of our major creditors had become bankers to the airline. The prospect of Virgin and Cityjet growing old together in a blissful union seemed even more unlikely and positively less desirable.

Early in the new year, Peter Ribeiro, our Commercial Director, managed to initiate dialogue with Air France, who were looking to upgrade their Paris/London City service from ATR 42 turboprops to jets. They had the option of contracting in a Fokker F-70 twin jet or go for a 146. We went after this half-open door with a vengeance. We devoured the comparative performance figures for operating both types of jet at London City. We knew the F-70 was extremely challenged in terms of short-field performance and we set about highlighting all of these weaknesses. We came close, but no cigar. They went with Air Littoral who operated the F-70. They would regret it very quickly, as the operational performance proved to be a disaster with a large number of flights being cancelled even for wet runways with stopping distance coming into question. In keeping with the trend of so many relationships which Cityjet attempted to forge, the Air France connection would be a slow burn, with an eventual big click.

Of course, we hadn't forgotten about Aer Lingus and the "on again, off again" set of proposals. We threw ourselves into the various route studies consistent with what our star-gazing with

Aer Lingus had thrown up two months earlier as potentially forming the basis of a co-branded European route development project. At a meeting very early in January, Aer Lingus confirmed that there was no realistic prospect of their Board approving an equity participation in Cityjet in the immediate months ahead. However, Aer Lingus did want to press on with the relationship and would like us to operate a Dublin/Manchester/Zurich service on their behalf and at no financial risk to Cityjet. The deal that emerged over the subsequent weeks was the Zurich operation plus a code share on Dublin/London City. The nice twist which we succeeded in negotiating was Aer Lingus TAB frequent flyer points for all passengers irrespective of whether they were travelling on Aer Lingus or Cityjet tickets.

There was only one problem. (There was always one problem.) We didn't have an aircraft to perform the contract on Zurich, which had to start on 1 April. Of course, we had anticipated needing one and we did our preliminary work on sourcing one in the preceding weeks. We took the chance on hiring additional crew in anticipation and we had them trained but we could not commit to the heavy deposit on another aircraft without the comfort of a signed contract with Aer Lingus. We had been close to consummation with them too many times before only to walk away empty-handed.

I was wrong to say there was just one problem. There was a second. To convince a leasing company to give you another aircraft required proving that you were in a state of reasonable financial good health and that you would be able to put up the deposit, pay the lease and the maintenance reserves to them. We had no secrets from BAe but they were not up for helping us on this one. Our credit with BAe, in every sense of the word, was spent. They had listened to too many "nearly there" stories around our relationship with Aer Lingus. We were crying wolf but nobody was interested. We were on our own.

In the middle of my frantic search for a serviceable BAe 146 aircraft to lease, my big moment on *The Late Late Show* arrived. A twenty-minute interview on live TV to an audience of one million is challenging. It was all the more so because Gay Byrne, although obviously very supportive of the entrepreneurial spirit of the little airline, naturally pursued some of the sticky issues like our competitive relationship with Aer Lingus, especially on Dublin/ Brussels. A lot was going through my head as I sweated under those lights and tried to look the nation in the eye through the lens of the camera. *I've got to stay on side with Aer Lingus*, I told myself, because of the deal we are trying to put together. *Don't kick the Government over the civil servants travel issue because you'll sound like a whinger.* I kept myself in check. And, of course, I still had to declare my admiration for Richard Branson because both Gay Byrne and the nation loved him. The reaction to the show was incredible. Aer Lingus were delighted I didn't give them a drubbing and they let us know. It certainly smoothed the way to conclude our Dublin/London City code share deal and the Dublin/Zurich contract.

In the months to follow, the image in the market of Cityjet was very much one of a highly professional small airline who "are in the business of flying people, not airplanes" — that's how I described what made us different in an answer to one of Gay Byrne's questions and the distinction seemed to resonate with many people.

Meanwhile, back to where and how to get our third aircraft for the Aer Lingus gig. I had learned of an interesting alternative to BAe for sourcing more 146s. US Air had purchased a smaller regional airline based in Charlotte, Carolina, some three years previously. Not being able to find a way around the pilots' scope agreement, they mothballed twenty-four BAe 146s in the desert. To shift these and other surplus aircraft in the airline's huge fleet, they set up US Air Leasing and based it in Washington DC.

In my ongoing long-range telephone dialogue with Richard Bartlett, the major shareholder in Air Wisconsin, I shared my problem about our acute shortage of aircraft and our lack of resources to get them. Richard suggested a way in which Air Wisconsin could make an indirect investment in Cityjet. The US Air

146s in the desert needed about US$2 million spent on each air-craft to render it fit for service. Air Wisconsin had a specialist 146 maintenance facility to look after their own large fleet. By under-taking the restoration to service work on aircraft which Cityjet would lease from US Air, Air Wisconsin could provide a certain proportion of this to US Air at no charge. In exchange, US Air would waive their requirement for a security deposit from Cityjet in respect of the leases. Richard calculated that the value of this type of deal would translate into about US$0.5 million per aircraft. It was a potentially workable idea. First US Air would have to agree to it and also Air Wisconsin would have to come to Dublin to carry out a due diligence on Cityjet to satisfy themselves on the risk. The latter would take time, to co-ordinate the timetables of the key people in Air Wisconsin. (The due diligence exercise did actually go ahead some six weeks later.) I didn't have that kind of time and any such proposition from Air Wisconsin to US Air, ahead of them formally confirming themselves as investors in Cityjet, would clearly define our credit risk as a basket case. In-stead I had to rely on going direct if I was to have any chance of getting the aircraft I needed for the Aer Lingus contract.

We had been conducting a telephone-based relationship-building exercise with US Air and had declared our interest in a specific BAe 146 which was only weeks away from completing a major overhaul after its long rest in the desert. With the Aer Lin-gus contract signed, I headed with Jane to New York for a few badly needed days off and of course an aircraft lease to clinch. I was really worried. Our balance sheet was not the sort that in-spired confidence with aircraft leasing companies. The Aer Lingus contract was for a twelve-month period and the minimum leasing term from US Air was thirty-six months. If I was to hold the reve-nue out of that contract as proof of how we were going to pay the lease rentals and maintenance reserves, it wouldn't really satisfy them. Again I was heading off for a negotiation which had to yield the right result. "Don't come home without an aircraft."

Chapter Nine

DANCING PARTNERS

I stood by the kerbside outside the terminal building at Washington Airport. The shuttle from La Guardia had been efficient and yet I had now been waiting almost an hour for my host, Jim Spalding of US Air Leasing. Around the bend he came in this beautiful red Mercedes SL 500. "Things must be going really well in the second-hand jet market," I quipped as we cruised to his office. "Oh no. You'll never guess, but I won this in a raffle," he laughed loudly. His office was interesting, with photos on the wall of Jim in the company of famous people including JFK and another one (separately) with Marilyn Monroe. Our Jim had been a fighter jock with the US Airforce in his younger years and from his demeanour he seemed to have found a way of converting to civil aviation without compromise to his swashbuckling style. We got on well but then Jim was selling and I was buying. I knew the tempo would change as soon as the finance guys got into the conversation. I didn't have to wait long. We went through the financials and I concentrated on the future projections. I emphasised the emerging relationship with Aer Lingus and how Cityjet would balance the revenues flow from our own risk routes with the certainty of contract revenue. I played up our institutional shareholder backing and I offered precious little in the way of historic figures. I had with me a pro forma balance sheet which put the best possible shape on our position but it still wasn't pretty. To get into any detailed discussion on that would be detrimental to our cause.

I was the one in selling mode now and they were the buyers. I knew the only chance I had was to be extremely confident and exploit their desire to open up a market for their desert-bound 146s against BAe Asset Management, the dominant player in the market. I pushed on the theme of getting one of their aircraft into Europe because that's where they had to aim to move the 146s. What better way, I argued, than to move with Cityjet, who were getting into bed with the Irish national carrier. And of course there would be no problem with our putting up the security deposit they were asking for. They wanted a few days to think it over. I pushed them. "OK, we'll give you an answer tomorrow. Call us from New York."

Meanwhile, back in Dublin the team was putting in place a short-term contract to wet lease in a BAe 146 to cover one of our two existing aircraft, which in turn would be released to start the Aer Lingus contract for the three weeks it would take for the US Air aircraft to be delivered from the maintenance facility in Calgary where it was undergoing its major overhaul. We tried to defer the start of the Aer Lingus contract, especially as they only finally signed on 14 March with a 1 April commencement. But they could not cut us any slack and we knew we had to run with it. The cost of wet leasing in for a few weeks was going to make a big dent in the deposit we had received from Aer Lingus against the contract.

Jane and I were staying in Fitzpatrick's Hotel in New York. It was a few days before St Patrick's Day but we wouldn't be staying for the festivities. But other guests in the hotel would, including Bertie Ahern and his partner, Celia Larkin. Bertie Ahern was leader of the opposition at the time and we had met on a few occasions in the previous two years. There had, indeed, been a recent occasion when Bertie and two of his party colleagues had travelled with Cityjet to a meeting in Whitehall with the then in opposition British Labour Party. I happened to be having an after-work drink in the bar in the departures terminal in Dublin, when I got a call from flight operations. "Bertie Ahern's group have just arrived very late for their flight at City but it's closed up and taxiing." I had been called earlier that day by his office to advise they were travelling and that it was vital they get back for an important engagement in Dublin that same evening. "Call him back to the ramp, shut down and open up for them," I instructed, as I visualised the indignation of the practically full load of mostly business people looking forward to getting home on time. But I knew his form and I wasn't surprised when I read the cabin supervisor's report of how Bertie had worked the plane, apologising to each and every one of our passengers and pressing the flesh. Everyone wants to meet the coming power and the mood of the time was that Bertie would be the next Taoiseach. We didn't get one letter of complaint.

Anyway, I made the call to US Air in Washington. It was a yes. Another step on the way to growing our way out of our problems.

We didn't hold our breath exclusively on Aer Lingus coming through for us, in terms of multi-route partnership opportunities in the first few months of 1996. We knew that we had to get more flying activity but only on a non-commercial risk basis. That meant contract flying anywhere we could get it and of course acquiring another aircraft to fulfil any such contract. Hugh Welburn of Virgin, who had remained a stalwart supporter of Cityjet's struggle to become a regional airline of consequence, had unearthed some promising contacts in Turin. A consortium of local banks and other parties had a desire to invest in a regional carrier who would commit to developing a route network for business people out of Turin to other cities, including London. Hugh and myself made two trips to Turin over February and March. We developed a detailed business plan. It all looked good. We were talking to what we thought was real money in the form of the banks and the local Government. What was in the air was a potential contract to operate scheduled services out of Turin with local money funding the operation. But it came to nothing. There was disagreement among the "partners" on

how to proceed, who would put up cash, etc. We detached ourselves from what was going to be a protracted talking shop.

We also had been talking with Alitalia since the previous autumn. We had been invited to their head office in Rome for talks
with very senior people on the serious subject of Cityjet operating
a twice-daily service for them on Milan to London City. The problem here was there was a more senior level who hadn't been clued
in to what was being looked at. Office politics in a large flag-
carrying airline was about to get us again. Alitalia eventually did
launch the service in question but with an Italian operator, Air
Azurra, flying Avro RJs (a BAe 146 with slightly more modern
engines and avionics but still with most of the same problems). In
an ironic twist, the Air Azurra aircraft bore Irish registration
marks through some clever tax-based leasing arrangement
through a Shannon-domiciled special purpose leasing company.

With the ink still wet on the contract with Aer Lingus to operate Dublin/Manchester/Zurich, we went into overdrive to get
completion on the US Air aircraft overhaul in Calgary. Every day
we could shorten the lead time to delivery would save us serious
money in hire-in costs of the wet-lease of the 146 from Titan Airways. By this stage our engineering department had grown its capacity to enable us to take over the line maintenance function we
had initially contracted out to Hunting Aircraft. We dispatched
two of our engineers to Calgary to pore through the paperwork on
the maintenance records and to monitor the progress of the overhaul. There were a number of specific challenges we were facing in
bringing this aircraft onto the Irish register. For a start, the fuel
gauges were calibrated differently to the European requirements
as laid down by the Joint Aviation Authority (JAA) and would
have to be changed. We also had a really silly situation in that the
anti-collision radar installed on the aircraft, which had been a
standard requirement of the US Federal Aviation Authority (FAA),
had to be removed. This compliance directive was ridiculous in the
extreme, particularly as the JAA had already signalled the forth-

coming introduction of anti-collision radar as a mandatory fit within the next few months. However, as it technically was surplus to requirements at this point in time, it would have to be removed at considerable expense in order to qualify for acceptance on the Irish register. True to form, some months later we had to reinstall the same system at further expense, to be compliant.

Air Wisconsin came to Dublin in early April for their due diligence exercise. We all thought it was still a good idea to see how far we could get in determining the prospect of becoming equity partners, especially as Aer Lingus were not showing signs yet of reaching for their cheque book. The few days with Richard Bartlett and the senior management team of Air Wisconsin went well. We even arranged for a three-way meeting with Aer Lingus for two reasons. We wanted to prove to the Americans that we had a reasonably good prospect of a long-term collaborative relationship with the national carrier, similar to the one they already had with United Airlines in the States. This was the model we knew would attract them most to taking a serious look at investing in Cityjet. We also needed to show Aer Lingus that we could leverage other third-party contacts to develop the capacity to be a regional carrier of significant size without a dependency on them alone. We wanted them to see they were not the only show in town and perhaps put a rocket up their backsides to complete what they had said they intended to do.

Air Wisconsin went home to consider what they might do in relation to getting involved with us. Our first aircraft from US Air arrived in late April in a basic Virgin Cityjet colour scheme, cloth seat covers instead of our customary leather and a very inadequate galley set-up. But it was a serviceable 146 and it would do a job for us in the short term while we figured out how to make the cabin configuration and service facilities more compatible with our other two aircraft.

If ever there was a time to go for breaking away from Virgin, it was now. We were flying the Dublin/Manchester/Zurich route on contract for Aer Lingus. We had a valuable code share agreement with Aer Lingus on Dublin/London City, with them guaranteeing the purchase of a significant number of business class seats, and our passengers could collect TAB points which were proving far more popular than Virgin frequent flyer miles. It was late April 1996 and our loan together with our deferred payment for services from Virgin were due for repayment from 1 May, and we still had no prospect of complying with that.

And then, just for a change, we got a bit of good luck. Branson handed us a golden opportunity on a plate. He had been toying with the notion of buying a Boeing 737 operation out of Brussels for a while when suddenly he went and did it. He was all over the papers. Virgin Express was to be the new low-cost carrier in Europe. Passengers on Virgin Express should not expect frills on short-haul routes. "If people want a meal, then they should go to a restaurant, but don't expect one on a Virgin Express flight", as a Virgin spokesman was quoted in one newspaper interview. This was it — time to pick a fight. I went for the gap and penned the strongest protestation I could scribe.

Spitting it out on paper, I told him that wearing the Virgin mantle carries with it very specific compliance responsibilities for Cityjet in meeting the Virgin product specification, as laid down unilaterally by Virgin. Such compliance demanded that Cityjet invested heavily in developing a short-haul product which met with the approval of Virgin. My letter went on to say that, in meeting the product standards set for us by Virgin, we were compelled to produce a quality of service that became recognised as the very best on Ireland/UK and Ireland/Europe routes. The impressive number of awards Cityjet had already won bore testimony to the quality of the service. I declared our complete astonishment at his very public redefinition of Europe's short-haul travel needs to be based solely on low fares. I speculated to him that the object of his new airline in Europe was clearly to win market share through low fares based on low-cost operations modelled on Valujet and Southwest. I challenged the rationale of his making a virtue out of offering his passengers a no-frills service and personally endorsing this American-style model of short-haul flying in the same market in which we operate. I rounded off my well-aimed missile by expressing the view that Virgin had damaged the Virgin short-haul product beyond repair by sowing the seeds in the public mind that Virgin was a low-cost low-fare operator of short-haul services rather than a quality services provider. I concluded by asserting that this would have a serious adverse affect on our sales and cash flow and therefore on the very viability of the company.

He was livid. Our ensuing phone conversation was heated. To compound the effect my letter had on him was the gossip he had picked up from the Virgin marketeers in Crawley. "I'm told you have one aircraft in Aer Lingus colours, one in ours and you've painted out the tail on another. I'm not stupid, I know what you are playing at," he shouted down the phone to me.

I could see why he was so mad at me and the idea of a multi-coloured fleet must have really got him going. I explained that we had no aircraft in Aer Lingus colours and the one with the tail painted out was actually the new one we had got from US Air. In keeping with Virgin branding guidelines, I did not paint the Virgin logo on for the transatlantic ferry flight as the aircraft was still bearing US registration marks. Also, we were awaiting the installation of galleys and leather seat covers and were not going to put a Virgin stamp on an inferior product. He was checked. He backed up quite a bit. We discussed the good sense of the code share with Aer Lingus as it was delivering more passengers than Virgin had been capable of doing so far and we both would benefit from this increase in revenue given that the franchise fee we paid to Virgin was a percentage of gross revenue. On the contract flying for Aer Lingus, he conceded that he had suggested this type of supplementary activity some two years earlier.

I likened what he was doing with Virgin Express to Ryanair. "How could passengers distinguish between two Virgin-tailed aircraft sitting side by side in Brussels and guess which one they would get a breakfast or a cup of coffee on?" I asked. "Why have we spent millions on developing a Virgin-style in-flight service which has won us every award in the book when you are in the media telling people they are fools to expect this type of service on short haul flights in Europe and they are spending fifty per cent too much on fares?" "Its not like Ryanair," he responded. "We are going to do it with style and panache just like South-west." He went on to defend the Virgin Express venture and to assure me that it would become clear to the market that it was quite a different proposition to Virgin Cityjet. I begged to differ and we agreed to disagree on the issue.

But the daggers were drawn; there would be no going back; we were going to split. The terms of the divorce were going to be the issue. More money for the lawyers — what's another round with Hardbottle and Lewis? For good order, I commissioned top London lawyers Clifford Chance to write our response to the pre-dictable terse demands for the price of freedom. It would drag on for a few weeks but the tunnel was nearing completion. It would get settled for stg£450,000 and not three times that, which was what Virgin had in their books as being owed by us.

Chapter Ten

ONE STOVE, MANY POTS, ALL BOILING

Virgin wasn't the only parting in the air as we headed towards summer. BAe had been fantastic in their support for us from the start but they had their commercial pressures too. Undoubtedly back in 1993 we had a compelling coincidence of objectives in getting a pair of 146s into the sky over the Irish sea. But things move on. Aer Lingus had by now taken delivery from BAe of a half dozen of the very same aircraft type they had snubbed previously. In a way, the original BAe objective had been achieved. I do believe, though, that Robin Southwell had a certain empathy with what we were trying to achieve and he became, to a degree, infected with our passion for getting there. I also think, more than most, he empathised with our troubled relationship with Virgin.

BAe had also committed themselves to supplying two more aircraft to NJS with a Qantas guarantee underpinning the deal. They wanted our original two aircraft, for which we had six months to run on the lease. We had wanted to extend for another three years. Their leverage in the persuasion stakes was of course the looming date of 1 May when we were obliged to start making heavy repayments on the loan and deferred payments for services, negotiated back in 1994. They pushed me to take their offer. Order two more from US Air now and they would leave cash on the table in the form of some debt forgiveness and the swapping out of galleys and leather seat covers, etc. They initially promoted this arrangement as being worth £1 million to Cityjet. The sting in the tail we feared would turn out to be the rigid enforcement of "return conditions" of the aircraft. This is where the lessee can really end up being screwed by a lessor pushing very hard on the condition of the aircraft at re-delivery.

US Air were starting to move aircraft out of the desert and had received orders for eight units from Debonair, a remarkably well-funded start-up founded by Franco Mancusola, a character as colourful as his name sounds. Titan Airways had taken two and Flightline, another specialist emergency 146 hire-in operator, were biting on a couple of aircraft. We reasoned it was better to take the BAe offer and return our two aircraft early, as if we waited another six months we might be in an even more difficult position to get replacements due to scarcity; also, the pressure to repay the BAe debt would sink us. We did the deal.

The net gain for Cityjet was very far south of the pumped-up indicative figure of £1 million but a considerable chunk of debt got wiped out and at least we had aircraft with fresh three-year leases.

US Air Leasing had a new President, Stewart Peebles, an amiable Scot with good previous experience with British Airways in aircraft procurement and leasing. From the off, I had a feeling I could do business with Stewart, as would prove to be the case over the following couple of years. The practice we had with getting the first US Air aircraft, which had brought us to a fleet strength of three units, was invaluable in heading off a lot of the problems with the overhaul of the next two in Calgary. We were getting good at this. By the time of our public declaration of independence as Cityjet with our own tail, which in keeping with our style of marketing, was set for 4 July, we had our fleet of three 146s from US Air, our original two from BAe having been returned in preparation for their next tour of duty down under with Qantas and our distant "friends", NJS.

The formula for navigating our way out of trouble was simple. At three aircraft, we were still too small to justify the fixed cost base of being an airline. To generate enough revenue and get over the gain line, we had to reach a point of critical mass in our flying operations. All of the emerging figures told us that was now at a minimum of four aircraft flying pretty much to the optimum of their capacity of hours per month. It had been an incredible struggle to get to three aircraft and the balance in our activity now stood at two aircraft flying two routes for our own commercial risk and one on risk-free terms operating for Aer Lingus. We also maximised our aircraft utilisation with a weekend charter series to Malaga and Faro in summer and Switzerland and Austria in the skiing season. Our next activity would also have to be a risk-free one, which is why we kept up the manic search for another airline customer. The Alitalia trail had gone cold yet again and the talks with the Turin local business interests weren't going anywhere. We also had a brief tryst with Air Malta who showed intense interest for a very brief period only for it to die as quickly as it started. But there was something different about the relationship we had been nurturing slowly with Air France.

We had lost out with their selection of a Fokker F-70 twin-jet operator to replace their turboprop service on Paris to London City. But the early experience they suffered with the limitations of the F-70 was awful. They were back at the table because they knew they needed a 146. The talking got down to detail very fast and the meetings in Paris were progressively being attended by more senior people from Air France. It was very evident we were moving up the food chain and this was their way of assessing us to see what we were made of. I had a sense that this growing relationship with Air France above all others was going to be vitally important to us going forward. But I also instinctively felt it would be a relationship that could only be built slowly over time, with the French giving us one contract at a time and us proving we were worthy of more. We got the nod by summer's end: five rotations per week-day on Paris CDG to London City, starting in late October. We needed a fourth aircraft and Stewart Peebles of US Air Leasing was top of my phone list.

Those summer months were fairly cluttered. We had the changeover of the two aircraft going back to BAe and the replacements from US Air coming in. We also had to swap the galleys and seats from one to the other, which meant more downtime and the consequent hiring-in of wet-leased aircraft from Titan. By now both sides in the Virgin/Cityjet divorce proceedings had taken to our respective trenches, donning our hard hats and only speaking to each other through salvos prepared and delivered by our respective lawyers. Conor McCarthy, Aer Lingus's Strategic Development Manager, had, in the preceding weeks, taken the local aviation community by complete surprise by making an astonishing move from Aer Lingus, where many would have tipped him as a potential future CEO, to join his archrival Michael O'Leary at Ryanair. I wasn't sure what this meant for our chances of ultimately getting Aer Lingus to invest in Cityjet. Meanwhile, I kept an informal dialogue going with them at what I felt was the appropriate level, especially to make sure they got the message that we were in the throes of severing the tie with Virgin and would very shortly be single again.

Just for good measure, there was another pot that had been simmering for a few weeks about to come to the boil. With all of the distractions of the past months and our desperate need for revenue generation opportunities, an enthusiastic charter broker who had been instrumental in obtaining a lot of charter contracts for us had introduced a daring concept to a senior member of our management team. The downside of my encouraging others to exercise their initiative was about to hit home very hard. Before I knew it, Cityjet was contractually committed to an elaborate summer season charter programme out of the UK to a number of Iberian Peninsula destinations. This was an amazingly complex piece of business.

The customer was a Portuguese airline, Sata Acores, who were one aircraft short to fulfil their summer charter programme for UK-based tour operators. They had a longstanding relationship with a specific UK tour operator, Avia Reps, who also owned a small charter airline. Avia Reps could only commit a Boeing 737 for the first eight weeks of the season and then they were sending it to New Zealand on a long-term engagement. Avia Reps approached our charter broker and together they came up with the notion of starting with the Avia Reps 737 and then rolling over onto a Yugoslav Airlines 737, seamlessly. The operation would be on Cityjet's airline licence but flown by a wet-leased Boeing 737 from Avia Reps for the first few weeks, to be replaced by another wet-leased 737 from Yugoslav Airlines. All flights would be on Cityjet's Irish designation of WX and flight operations and ground support would be managed from Dublin. Additionally, Cityjet would recruit, train and manage Portuguese cabin crew to operate on the Yugoslav aircraft. The margin for us was healthy and on paper the deal would generate good profits. But the boys hadn't thought it the whole way through and omitted to check things out informally with the Irish regulatory authorities. Yugoslavia of course in 1996 wasn't exactly flavour of the month and UN sanctions were biting hard. A consequence of this was a grossly under-utilised fleet available for hire. We were blind to the political mood in Europe translating into a concerted resistance by many states to assisting in any way the commercial recovery of any Yugoslav-owned business. So there was an issue.

On the eve of the planned transfer from the UK aircraft, the Department of Transport in Dublin refused to grant Cityjet permission to wet-lease the Yugoslav aircraft on the grounds of their being outside of the EU-controlled Joint Aviation Authority's jurisdiction. The safety card was played against us despite the fact that Yugoslav Airlines met the full compliance requirements in standards laid down by ICAO and were prepared to submit to a full audit and inspection by the Irish authorities or any other nominated body. We were goosed. The flying programme called for two rotations per day out of the UK from Thursday through Monday every week. It was all in Cityjet's name and we were contractually obliged to fulfil our obligations. It was a nightmare. We were scrabbling around every week for aircraft to hire-in and usually at prices that left no margin for us at all. The charter market is vicious and our plight was becoming known. Cityjet could be scalped on price because they would have to pay.

I now had to get involved on a full-time basis to try to solve this mess. In reality, what had happened was a hanging offence but perhaps my style of trusting people to do the right thing and not over-extend us was as much at fault as those who should have been hung for getting us into this stupid situation. Valuable time and energy was being burned at a time when I needed to complete the separation from Virgin, try to get Aer Lingus into bed and sign Air France for a major contract. Myself and Aidan Keane, our new financial controller, headed for Lisbon to sort out a deal with Sata Acores. We had had inconclusive talks with Avia Reps who had been appointed by the Portuguese to represent their interests and stick Cityjet to the letter of the signed contract they kept waving in front of us. It was a long hot day and by five o'clock I thought we had it clinched; a good compromise in the circumstances that would cost us money, we could walk away and get on with the other pressing issues that were more immediately life-threatening. Not to be. There was a man in the room who fulfilled the potential he had been showing all day to be the wrecker of the proposal that I was certain his boss wanted to accept. "We've a plane to catch. Let's make our respective lawyers even richer," I proclaimed as we left for the airport, angry, tired and utterly frustrated.

The following week I gave the directive to cease the sub-chartering operation. I sent a fax to Sata Acores and suggested they should look after their UK tour operators themselves. More legal paper started flying as they began to seek damages of stg£0.5 million. Right now, I could do nothing about it but rely on our lawyers to stall and procrastinate while I got back to the other dirty dishes that I could do something about. At least the high-pressure tension in our flight operations room of trying to sort out sub-charters was gone, and that was a big relief.

Sometimes when you're in the groove of daily battles you begin to see things more clearly. You lose your inhibitions because when you are embattled and taking flak from all sides you develop a sense that the only worthwhile pursuit is to try to win. You toughen up because you know your opponents can't hurt you anymore than they already have. You get to a state of believing that no further damage can be inflicted. You become impregnable to incremental damage. I absolutely believed that Cityjet would survive and I was impatient for the next chapter to begin.

Virgin was the blocker. I had just got off our early morning flight at London City when I dialled Richard Branson's private residence on Holland Park, which immediately adjoins his office. To my surprise, he answered the phone himself from his bath, or so he told me. "If I had known it was you I would not have answered," he growled down the phone. I didn't care what he thought, I was going to sort this out. The way things were going with the lawyers, I told him, we would both have large bills to pay and an ongoing messy situation between us, with the ever-present risk of media attention on our squabble. "I want this sorted now, Richard, and all it takes is for you to call off your lawyers and sit down with me or get someone else I can relate to in your organisation to hammer out a quick resolution, and lets get on with life." After a moment of silence, he responded: "I suppose you're right. I don't want it dragging on. I'll get Frances to talk to you and get a deal worked out." And that was it. Within two weeks, we had a detailed and beautifully short document. It would cost us £0.45 million to walk away from a debt of stg£1.2 million. They would assist us in migrating to the Aer Lin-

gus reservations system, Astral, and arrange for an orderly disen-
gagement and a unified story for the media.

Life in Cityjet wasn't just about these strategic issues. Living in
the now threw up its own curious challenges. One such scenario
was unfolding and, quite typically, it was a Friday evening. We
heard from the captain of our early evening flight into City, where
the July temperature was high and about to get higher. We had a
problem — nothing wrong with the aircraft, but our captain had
been denied permission to disembark our passengers. Seemingly
during the final phase of the flight our senior cabin crew member
advised the captain that a young child being accompanied by her
aunt had become ill. The aunt was frightened that the child might
be suffering from meningitis, as there had been an incidence of it
in her playschool the previous week. The captain radioed ahead to
request an ambulance to meet the flight and take the child to hospital to have things checked out. The aircraft came to a halt, the
child was whisked off with her aunt to the waiting ambulance and
then, to the astonishment of our crew, the airport management ordered the passengers making their way across the apron to get
back on board immediately. The doors were closed and our passengers were imprisoned. Having got over the initial stage of disbelief, our operational management team and myself back in
Dublin decided to contact our medical officer to obtain a professional opinion as to the risks to our passengers from the transmis-
sion of meningitis. We spoke by phone with the airport director at
City, to be told in no uncertain terms that he was acting on the advice of the London Port Authority to quarantine our passengers to
prevent the spread of the illness. We remonstrated with this man,
to no avail. Meanwhile our evening schedule was about to go out
the window. We had a full load, as you would expect on a Friday,
waiting to board this aircraft, plus a further two flights to be performed by this same plane before evening's end. Among our passengers caught up in this "near hijack" situation was Formula One
World Champion, Damon Hill and family. By now, almost ninety

minutes had elapsed since our flight had touched down. We took the initiative of finding out where the child with the suspected meningitis had been taken and we followed up with numerous calls until we finally spoke directly with the doctor who had examined her — and had discharged her, having determined there was nothing more than travel sickness at the root of the problem.

We immediately presented this "fresh evidence" to the airport director, who still refused to allow our passengers off the plane. At that point, I contacted our captain on his cell phone and instructed him to lead his passengers off the aircraft immediately and to use force if apprehended by airport personnel. Seeing that we meant business, the airport people sensibly did nothing to prevent disembarkation; however, they refused to allow our passengers and crew to leave the confines of a lounge they had ushered them into. They were insisting that everyone be inoculated against meningitis before they could be allowed leave. We went ballistic and refused point blank to even allow a suggestion of such a measure be put to our passengers. Incredibly, it took another thirty minutes or so before the management at City Airport, obviously high on the adrenaline of a "real emergency", relented and stopped ruining the rest of our passengers' day. The cost of the disruption to our passengers awaiting our "liberated" aircraft would, as always, be for the account of Cityjet, without even as much as an apology from the airport management for the nonsense they had caused.

Coming up with the money to pay Virgin was painful, with some of our shareholders agreeing to put up some more cash, as did Luke and myself, to discharge the payment. The feeling of being free from the shackles of Virgin was wonderful and the mood throughout the company was fantastic. We re-launched as only our brilliant marketing team knew how, in style. The coverage in the media was encouraging and the good wishes from our regular passengers was uplifting. Morale was never higher but sadly that could do nothing for our liquidity position, which was getting acute. With the change over from BAe to US Air Leasing, we had tied up large cash deposits on the three aircraft and we were positioning ourselves to order a fourth for the anticipated Air France contract starting in October.

We were also having a very bad run with engines and, notwithstanding that we had now been enrolled in the Engine Maintenance Cost Protection programme (EMCP) with Allied Signals, we were hurting through a high incidence of component failures, resulting in the hiring-in of spare engines. In a typical review meeting of that time with senior people from the Allied Signals engine overhaul facility in Luton, we discussed the status of four of our engines in varying states of completion in their overhaul. Given that we had twelve engines on-wing in our fleet of three aircraft and two spare engines, to have four in the shop was not helpful. Two of those engines had only recently been removed from wing, with only 102 and 109 cycles consumed respectively since having returned to us from the Luton shop. There was an enormous quality assurance issue here and it was costing us a fortune. On top of this, we had a discussion on another engine we had just removed in Dublin, which Allied Signals were trying to declare as being out of warranty. This would cost us US$450,000 in parts not covered under EMCP. There was a lot of tough talking done that day, but it was straight and focused on getting a result based on trade-offs that everybody could live with.

Chapter Eleven

NOT ON MY WATCH!

A er Lingus were awfully quiet. We had been flying free of Virgin for a number of weeks and our code share with Aer Lingus on London was working extremely well. We had been operating for Aer Lingus on Zurich for four months with no major problems. But where was the sign of a move towards them becoming an investment partner? What was happening about the development of new European routes under the sub-brand of *"Cityjet, an Aer Lingus Partner"*? Nothing. Not a word. Our directors were getting nervous about the worsening cash position of the airline. We met with the shareholders one by one to seek more support. We held two extraordinary shareholder meetings in close succession to outline the position and to appeal for more investment. The response was resoundingly clear. There would be no more cash unless I could produce an airline partner. They were disappointed at the lack of progress with Aer Lingus in respect of the potential prospect of them becoming an investor in Cityjet. Feeling the heat, I bowed to the pressure, which turned out to be a grave tactical error. I went to see Aer Lingus. I acquainted them with the aggressive moves being made by Air UK, a wholly owned subsidiary of KLM, to become the dominant carrier at London City Airport. I suggested that it was not beyond the bounds of probability that Air UK could turn their attention to the Dublin route and that wouldn't be good for any of us. I proposed that if the political and industrial relations climatic conditions were still not right for Aer Lingus to make their investment move on Cityjet, perhaps they might consider buying the Dublin/London City route from us and then place a contract with Cityjet to operate it on their behalf? Very bad move by me.

They took ten days to mull it over and the firm "no" came down the phone on cue. Now I was really worried. Were they counting the days we had to live? Was it that obvious? Had we been sucked in and now were we being blown out? I don't know what really happened. I don't think the original move was to lead us up a false alley. But things change. Maybe there were emerging forces within Aer Lingus, not readily visible to us, who didn't see taking a stake in Cityjet as a tactically clever move. Perhaps their lawyers frightened them off with the prospect of an EU backlash to investing in another carrier so soon after receiving state aid.

In all probability, what really killed any hope of a deal was the length of time that had elapsed from the initiation of the idea. We had candidly shared the view at our first meeting that day in the Shelbourne Hotel, some twelve months previously, that such deals have a certain life, after which the moment passes if it doesn't get done. Very prophetic, as it turned out. Original intentions may well have been good but a tiredness crept in and the enthusiasm waned.

Now we really were talking about weeks to live. I started on a series of talks with our major creditors. I was brutally open with them about our struggling situation and asked for support in slowing down payments. I needed to acquaint them with our position and to make it clear they were at risk for payment as they continued to supply us. This was essential in order to satisfy ourselves as directors of the company that we had the acquiescence of our senior creditors while we continued to avail of their services with no certainty of their being paid in full. I also undertook to keep them fully informed on any progress with potential airline investment partners.

But where was I going to find one? I couldn't go to Air France, who had now committed to the Paris/London City contract, and ask them to rescue us. It was too early in that relationship. Air

Wisconsin had offered to our shareholders to come in and occupy executive positions in the company for three months and, if they liked it, they might invest. That, quite correctly, was flatly rejected. No money in, no control.

I was a pretty depressed airline CEO, with probably not much longer to go in that particular job category, as I arrived in Edinburgh on an early September evening. I was joining the other 146 operators, who were all attending the annual BAe Presidents Club gathering on the eve of the Farnborough Show. The dinner in the castle on the Firth of Forth was impressive and the chat with the usual suspects was the same old banter. Back at the hotel, I was introduced to Hans Kallenius, the recently appointed CEO of Malmo Aviation. We had had very brief peripheral encounters with Malmo prior to this, starting with the fact we had employed one of their senior training captains at the very outset. We also had had an informal meeting with their owner, which had come to nothing at that point. However, Malmo Aviation was a compellingly interesting regional operator.

Hans was an impact player. When you met him, you knew you were dealing with a force. A friend of the Crafoord Wiklund family who owned the airline, Hans had been brought in to run the company and provide support for the thirty-year-old Stefan Wiklund, who now wished to act as chairman and vacate the CEO role. Hans wasn't of the airline community, his previous role being CEO of Pripps, the brewing company. A smart if somewhat conservative dresser, he cut a good figure belying his fifty-something years. I spoke very openly to him about my quest for an airline partner. His English was impeccable and his charm disarmingly effective. He displayed a very well-educated background and a very sharp mind. We got on well. He asked good questions and took detailed notes. A clinical operator, I thought. We arranged to meet in London in two weeks' time. I was intrigued at the encounter but at this stage I would not allow myself to get excited about the prospects of salvation.

Two days later, I was having an in-depth exploratory meeting with the Air UK CEO, Henny Essenberg, who had been implanted by KLM following their purchase of Air UK from their private British owners. I wanted to find out more of his intentions in relation to expansion at London City and what room there was for co-operation with Cityjet. I didn't know where this might lead but I had to get in front of potential airline partners and try to make something happen.

At the next meeting with Hans Kallenius and Stefan Wiklund in London, we made some progress. They were interested in looking at how the two airlines might be put together. We stayed in touch by telephone over the next couple of weeks and then Aidan Keane and myself went to Sweden to make the business case for Malmo investing in Cityjet. We worked late into the night at the very new age but comfortable offices in downtown Malmo. The format was workshop. We covered all of the potential reasons for coming together and analysed the potential synergies vigorously. Malmo had ten 146s and we had four. By combining the operations, it would not take long to be up to twenty aircraft overall. The atmosphere between us was good, especially if we were taking Hans Kallenius as the barometer, but Stefan was quiet and reserved. I wasn't sure if that was his usual form or if I should read negative things into it. The mood over dinner was getting even more positive. The chemistry was clicking into place. Coming back to Dublin, Aidan and myself were confident we were on the brink of a breakthrough. We certainly needed to be.

Dermot Desmond had very pointedly said to me on our two or three previous chance encounters in airports that he would let the summer finish out before he would begin applying pressure as a major creditor to get us to sort ourselves out. He wasn't joking. He made his move by inviting us to appoint his company, International Investment Underwriters (IIU), as special advisers with full access to all our financial information and an authority to talk to potential investors. This was an invitation where refusal was tantamount to helping him to pull the rug. We reluctantly surrendered and gave him a letter of appointment on 1 October. Now things had the potential to get outside of our control.

We were hardly back twenty-four hours from our trip to Sweden when the call came through from Hans Kallenius. He was disappointed, but the family had decided against taking things any further with Cityjet. I was floored. It wasn't that any firm commitments or declarations of intent had been given in Malmo, yet the manner of the talks had led me to put a really high probability on something positive happening. Now it really was moving rapidly away from me.

It was Friday 4 October and in a move of desperation, Luke and myself arranged for an evening meeting with Aer Lingus. We put our cards on the table about our financial position. We told them our shareholders were reluctant to put in more cash without us securing an airline partner for a minority equity position. We went back over the history of the dialogue between the two airlines over the past year that was pointing towards a potential investment by Aer Lingus for a minority stake in Cityjet. Battle-hardened as I had become and long since having given up on the notion of Aer Lingus representing our hope for a sound future, even I was shocked at the clinical nature of the response we got across the table. It was made absolutely clear to us that Aer Lingus would not make an investment in Cityjet and that they could not help our airline in any way. The concluding suggestion that in many ways it would "probably suit" Aer Lingus if Cityjet went bust was unambiguous confirmation of where exactly our relationship stood. Numbing stuff.

If there was a time for self-questioning, for considering throwing in the towel, this was it, more so than on any of the other many previous occasions. What was it about Cityjet? Why had we been spurned by a litany of prospective partners?

Was it me and my style of engagement with these "prospects", or was it simply that the business wasn't viable? Was I so arrogant that I knew better than the "experts" in the industry who looked at us and walked on by? Had I become obsessive in such an unhealthy way that I simply would not, could not let it drop? Yet we had endured. It had been so tough to get the company into the air in the first place and ten times tougher to keep it up there ever since. The more I asked myself why we were still alive, the more I saw the answer. This was an extraordinary little company where people didn't just come to work. Cityjet had become, for the people involved with it, a way of life. In Cityjet, each staff member could express themselves through the vital part they each played in delivering to the passenger the best possible service every day in spite of the challenges thrown up from every quarter. At our meetings — be they operational, engineering, financial, marketing or administration — there were always problems being discussed and always solutions coming forward from the people around the table. It was this incredibly positive atmosphere where invention happened and good humour prevailed.

It didn't matter whether the bombs came from competitor action, unfavourable support from travel agents, technical failures through flawed design, sloppy vendor service, dirty tricks in the marketplace or the consequence of the sheer comparatively small resource size of the airline. There was a sense among these people that winning against the odds was the only acceptable outcome. And our customers were pleased with us. We were doing a lot right. And our senior creditors, with whom we had endless rows over the quality and cost of services being provided to us were, de facto, keeping us in business for the time being. There was, in effect, a broader community here that wanted us to survive.

Up to this point, I had never felt desperate or clueless about where to look next for the hint of a scent towards home. But now, in this place of complete hopelessness, with absolutely no visible way out of the lack of financial resources to continue, I really put it up to myself. I resolved very solemnly, and maybe quite madly, that the ship was not going down — and certainly not on my watch. I had a responsibility to the shareholders who believed in us and to the totally committed staff and management. I had a responsibility to the market that said "yes" to our service and to the aviation industry partners who were taking risks by continuing to supply us. Leadership is not about running out onto the pitch on a fine sunny day with your team trooping behind you. It's about being twenty points down and playing against the wind and rain with only fifteen minutes to go in the match and knowing you have to do something about it. Leadership is where quitting is not an option and getting a result is a must-do.

I was driving back out the motorway from yet another meeting in town keeping shareholders abreast with the ever-gloomier picture, with still no sign of the cavalry coming over the hill, when I pulled over and stopped the car. I don't know why I got the impulse to dial Hans Kallenius in Malmo, but when he came on the line, I launched into my finest moment of articulation as to why I thought he was missing out on a most incredible opportunity that spelled synergy, no matter what you did with the letters in English or Swedish. It was a long conversation and he laughed at my direct and very impassioned delivery. But he was not mocking me. He was buying into this. Yes, he would go back and talk to Stefan and his brothers one more time. Why not? I was exhausted when I got to the office. Completely drained by the time I sat down behind my desk, I did nothing for an hour or more.

Later that evening a call came from Malmo. "How are you getting on with attracting more Irish investment?" was the opening question from Hans. *This is positive*, my intuition yelled at me. I had been in exploratory discussions in Dublin with Paul Coulson's Yeoman International Investment vehicle regarding the prospect of their becoming involved as shareholders in Cityjet. By now, the appetite for further investment by some of the existing shareholders was zero while a handful were still interested provided we found an airline partner who would invest. Yeoman, while not committing themselves, had indicated they might look more closely at us if we produced the airline partner. I was straight with Hans and told him if Malmo came in I was confident of getting Irish money too. "But what are you telling me, Hans?" I nervously asked. "The family have agreed to reconsider and I would like to meet with some of your Irish shareholders," he responded. Hans went on to say that they were thinking in terms of a substantial minority stake and that their involvement, if any, would be contingent on me getting more Irish funding for the majority.

My nerve ends were in a mess. I was full of anxiety about losing this potential victory, which I had absolutely no right at this point to even think might happen. The following days were frantic. Deeper talks with Yeoman and of course the rounding up of the existing shareholders to test just how much they would go on a restructured Cityjet. I also embarked on yet another round of visits to BAe, Allied Signals and IIU to ensure nothing silly might happen through trigger happiness just as we might be about to pull off a re-capitalisation. I needed the flow of aircraft spares and engines to be uninterrupted and I didn't need London City Airport parking a fire truck in front of one of our aircraft for non-payment of charges. That kind of event would rapidly convert an investment rescue opportunity into a basket case.

I got home about 7.30; my response over the kitchen table as to how my day had gone was interrupted by the dreaded sound of my mobile, which seemed to always herald trouble. It was operations and there was a problem with our final evening departure out of Dublin for City. The passengers could be re-protected with Aer Lingus to Heathrow but there would be an issue of getting our London City departing passengers home. I enquired about our last flight out of City to Paris and whether it would be possible to turn that around quickly and send it back to London to lift our Dublin-bound load home. The ops controller went away to do a lot of calculating and re-scheduling. Taking the flight back from Paris to pick up passengers at London and bring them to Dublin would mean that aircraft and crew would be in the wrong place for tomorrow morning. However, if the aircraft with the technical problem at Dublin could be fixed, then we could position it with another crew to Paris in the dead of night and everything should balance out. Sounds easy, but these last-minute changes to scheduling are a nightmare for everybody. Without the incredibly positive attitude of our ops staff, engineers and crew, such innovative resolution of problems would never have happened.

Anyway, we set up for the London to Paris aircraft to turn around out of CDG and head back to City. There was a worry that we would be up against the curfew at City and so I phoned the airport's CEO, who was at home. I explained what we were at and he promised to intercede with his air traffic control officer on duty in the tower to co-operate with the rescue plan. We picked up a small air traffic slot delay in getting off from CDG but our aircraft was on its way and our patient passengers at City were kept fully informed by our station manager. Happy that everything was going to work out, I relaxed into the evening at home when yet again the dreaded shrill of my ringing phone punctured my haven. It was operations in Dublin to tell me they had just received a communication from our inbound flight from Paris to City to the effect that when on final approach the runway lights were shut off by the air traffic controller and the airport declared closed. Our aircraft was now diverting to Heathrow and we had to find a way of getting our very anxious passengers at City to join up with the plane on the other side of London. Now not only would we have seriously aggrieved passengers to take care of but the crew we had "burned" on the Paris to City to Dublin rescue mission would be out of duty hours tomorrow morning. It was going to be a long night. (But not for the air traffic controller, who would make it home on schedule.)

The first meeting with those of our shareholders who were prepared to re-invest and with the Swedes took place over breakfast in the Conrad Hotel in Dublin. It was a businesslike yet warm first encounter and it felt like it was going somewhere. Many more meetings took place but none more crucial than the afternoon I awaited the arrival of Paul Coulson at Copenhagen airport. He was en route from Poland back to Dublin and had agreed to break his journey to meet with the Malmo people. Copenhagen was a good option for everybody and so the coffee sales were up that afternoon. We covered a lot of ground and there was a mutual liking of the cut of the respective jibs. Of course, there were reserved positions and talk of conditions precedent but I could tell that this deal was going to happen. There would be occasions when we needed to hold our collective breaths over the following couple of weeks, like when the Swedes came to Dublin in the company of a wealthy entrepreneur compatriot sporting his own executive jet and his legal adviser. The boys from Malmo were hoping to get this investor to go in with them on the Cityjet deal, as they were working on an ultimate exit strategy for Malmo Aviation.

By buying into Cityjet, Malmo would develop a true international dimension which would enhance the perceived value of the two airlines moving towards integration. This guy had already invested in a helicopter operation. He came, he kicked the tyres for a day and declined; but to their credit Malmo pressed on as if this was merely a blip. The target capital amount for restructuring the company was IR£4 million and the Swedes were up for forty per cent. We had firm commitments from one of our institutional shareholders and two of our private investors, Brendan McDonald and Mike Murphy. Paul Coulson and Yeoman were ready to come in, but we still needed about £0.5 million. Time was short. I was introduced to a successful man who I had only known previously by his reputation in business. He was fantastic in as much as he was tough on the questioning but extremely straight in declaring what he was thinking. He said "yes" and committed £0.25 million. The line was in sight. One of our private shareholders did some Trojan work in conditioning two of his associates to listen, and we were there.

Except! . . . except for the "car wash".

One man and his dream: Pat Byrne at Dublin Airport

Pat Byrne with one of the Marchettis in Texas, 1991

The Delivery: just after landing in Dublin on-board EI-JET,
23 December 1993

Pat Byrne and Luke Mooney: "Now we've got the airplane,
will any passengers show up?"

Jane checking out
the leather, on the
delivery of EI-JET,
23 December 1993

First "Wings" group of cabin crew, January 1994,
including Paddy O'Reilly (first left), Pearse Gilroy (second left)
and Linda Corr, Head of Cabin Crew (first right)

The undeniable climb capability of the BAe 146

Left: Launch Day,
10 January 1994

Right: Charlie
McCreevy, then
Minister for Trade
and Tourism, and
Richard Branson
counting engines
before take-off of the
inaugural flight to
London City Airport,
10 January 1994

EI-CTY and EI-JET at London City Airport, early 1994

Impact players at London City

EI-CTY lifts off from London City Airport

Sharon Ryan with the awards for Airline of the Year and
Best Ireland to London Airline, in our first year of operation, 1994

Happy First Birthday! Pat Byrne, Natalie O'Brien and then
Minister for Transport and Communications, Michael Lowry

4 July 1996: Independence Day from Virgin

"The Right Stuff"

Playing with the big boys

The Franco-Irish liaison: October 1996,
applying the Air France colours at Shannon

Teamwork

The first Irish adoption of a Chinese child, Emma Mulligan, with her delighted parents Cyril and Susan, arriving back in Dublin with Cityjet, pictured with Vanessa Hennessey

Taking delivery of our first Saab 2000 in March 1998

Rollout of a Cityjet Saab 2000 in Air France livery

A man with a brand for all seasons

Passing on the baton to Jacques Bankir, 31 March 2000

The irrepressible, irreplaceable and original one-off,
Captain Kevin Barry

Au Revoir

The opening of the new Cityjet offices in Swords, 3 March 2003

At the opening of the new Cityjet offices: Pat Byrne, Minister for Transport Seamus Brennan, and Geoff White, the new Cityjet CEO

In the new Cityjet offices: Hugh Rodgers, Financial Director,
Russ Kane, Pat Byrne and Geoff White, CEO

Flying into the future: Geoff White, CEO, Brian Tyrell, Chief Pilot,
and Pat Byrne, Chairman

Feeding time at Le Hub, Paris CDG: The Cityjet Flying Geese

Chapter Twelve

THE CAR WASH

Up to then I hadn't heard the term "car wash" in the context in which it was used by Paul Coulson that November afternoon in my office. The lawyers from McCann Fitzgerald were preparing to give me my office back, as they had planned to decamp back to their own territory, having completed all of the due diligence work they were performing on behalf of the new investors. Paul Coulson and Hans Kallenius returned from the corridor, where they had been for a few minutes. "There's just one more thing to be done before the investment can go ahead," Paul said. I wasn't perturbed, as I had spent the past weeks being asked to produce "one more document" or answer "one more question". But this was very different. "Hans and I are in agreement. We want you to put the company through 'the car wash' before we put in our money." I was perplexed. "What the hell is 'the car wash'?" I asked, with genuine innocence and ignorance. It turned out that what the investors were proposing was what they defined as "a pre-packaged examinership". Similar, but different in many respects, to Chapter 11 and fundamentally different to "under administration", as pertains in the UK, this was a unique arrangement under Irish law. Examinership was designed to give companies an opportunity to restructure themselves provided the vital components were present e.g. creditor approval, fresh investment and a viable plan going forward.

I couldn't take this in. I had thought in my naivety that the investors were going to come in and take over from where those of our original shareholders not going forward had left off. But, a few sentences into this conversation with my new potential shareholders, it was abundantly clear that they had no appetite for their cash being eaten in paying for "past sins", as they put it. They told me they recognised my strong relationships with the senior creditors in securing their support to keep us in the game this long. Now it was time for me to convert that support into a tangible commitment to write off substantial chunks of what we owed them in exchange for future business from a stronger and expanding airline going forward. *They can't be serious*, I thought to myself.

The images flashing through my mind were of the excruciatingly difficult conversations I had been having with Allied Signals, with whom we had a love/hate relationship over the money we owed and the less-than-satisfactory service they were giving in the overhaul of engines. The really tough talks were with BAe, who could bring down the guillotine on our airframe support account any day and shut off our supply of spare parts, such was the extent of our arrears. And there was London City and Dermot Desmond, whom I continuously managed to keep at bay; I just didn't know how he would react to what I was being asked to seek. There were other important creditors as well, the most notable of course being US Air who provided us with our entire fleet. But they had been okay up to now, as we kept the lease payments absolutely up to date and they had our deposits covering three months' rentals per aircraft. But examinership was going to be a problem even with US Air. As with all aircraft leases, any compromised situation for a lessee with creditors can be an automatic trigger of default on the lease. *And what about the staff?* My mind raced on. *How am I going to tell them not to worry? Your jobs are safe. This is just a process we have to go through. And the media? The media will have a field day and the passengers will walk and what's the bloody point of it all?* I continued to indulge myself in my head only. *Get a grip*, I told myself. *Not the time nor the place for an outburst*, I counselled myself wisely.

"Okay, let's take a look at what needs to be done," I said, trying to conceal my abject terror at the prospect of what lay ahead of me.

I had to perform many difficult and unpleasant tasks in bringing Cityjet to this point, but none more trying than having to face this particular music with each of our major creditors. I had kept them informed about our efforts to secure fresh investment and they had every expectation that with a re-capitalisation of Cityjet they would see some semblance of normality return to our payments pattern for services supplied. Twenty-five cents in the dollar is a great discount in anyone's eyes. But when you reverse it and tell your creditor, who has kept faith with you through the very bad days because he believed in you, that he has to swallow the other seventy-five cents, then that's putting the trust you have built up to the ultimate test. But that's where I found myself in the ensuing days. I had to tell them my own shareholding was getting hammered too and that certainly helped as I wasn't standing before them and asking them to take all the pain.

"Who else has agreed to this 'arrangement'?" was pretty much the stock question of the moment. No one wanted to be first to go along with the plan and yet if someone didn't, then nobody would, an all-too-familiar "Catch 22" scenario which seemed to track me on every turn with this job. I kept up the pressure, which meant doubling back to who I saw yesterday and the day before until eventually I brought the three legs of the stool together. We had consensus and all parties felt that each was carrying an equitable share of the load. I got an insight into how Henry Kissinger must have felt in the days when he was pioneering shuttle diplomacy.

Now we had the buy-in from all of those who could close us down — namely, BAe, Allied Signals and London City. Well, almost all; we had yet to deal with US Air Leasing and I was about to test my gut feeling that their President Stewart Peebles was a pragmatic soul. I called him and asked him where he'd be on Friday, two days later. "As its Thanksgiving over here, I'll be at home in Washington. Why do you ask?" he replied, the curiosity plain in his tone. "I need to come and see you and I want to bring our new investors with me. Its critically urgent," I added. "We need a meeting. We can be in JFK by 9.30 and then we can get the shuttle out of La Guardia." Stewart never flinched, at least as far as I could tell over the phone. In his laconic Scottish voice, he said, "What time could you be in the Plaza in Manhattan? And I'll come up from Washington to meet you."

Concorde was an incredible thrill. Paul Coulson and myself met up with Stefan Wiklund at the check-in at Heathrow, having hopped on the first flight out of Dublin that Friday morning. The first thing that hits you when you board this amazing aircraft is the smell of fuel and the compact shape of the long narrow cabin. With a number of cabin dividers, they manage to create a very intimate atmosphere and when seated you feel like you are in an executive jet as you are only conscious of a small number of seats in your section. Even though they give you a warning, the pressure that forces you back into your seat as the aircraft rapidly accelerates to take-off speed is impressive. And then what feels like the almost vertical angle of climb lets you know that this is no ordinary flight on a conventional aircraft. In level cruise, the things that struck me most were being able to see the curvature of the earth as we rocketed on at 60,000 feet and the constant dolphin-like flexing motion of the cabin floor. The aircraft is flying so fast that the friction it produces as it cuts through the air at twice the speed of sound heats up the skin and the interior wall of the cabin becomes very hot. The shame of it all was that, in three hours from take-off, this extraordinary flying experience was all over as we taxied to the ramp at JFK. It was 9.00, my third breakfast time in my third city on the same day.

Manhattan was packed with people on holiday. This was Thanksgiving weekend and New Yorkers were out in family mode and it seemed they all were having morning coffee at the Plaza. Stewart arrived a couple of hours later and ushered us into the restaurant for an early lunch. We came right to the point. I introduced him to Paul and Stefan and explained that they represented the Irish and Swedish shareholders who were committed to re-capitalising Cityjet. However, it was a precondition that the airline undergo an examinership process to arrive at an accommodation with creditors and lighten the burdening debts that would otherwise mitigate against recovery. We assured him we would keep paying the normal lease rentals on the aircraft but we needed his co-operation in not invoking the default clause on account of our compromised position with creditors. In short, we needed to fly our way through examinership in a business-as-usual manner and having aircraft was pretty essential to achieving this. It didn't take him long to make up his mind. He engaged with Paul and Stefan about their bona fides. He looked for an assurance that he would be kept absolutely in the loop throughout the critical weeks of examinership. He sought an undertaking that he would be first to know if it appeared the airline was not going to emerge successfully out of examinership. We shook hands.

The next crucial party to get on-board was the Irish Aviation Authority and the Department of Transport. All of what we were trying to accomplish would come to zero if we had our licence revoked. More plain speaking and a direct plea for support. It helped to have the new shareholders with me at the meeting. The authorities were responsive and they didn't mess around with slow "maybes". They understood the need for speed and no ambiguity. The key was being able to give a solemn undertaking that enough cash would be available throughout the period of examinership to ensure no compromise to the continued safe operation of the airline. I also reassured them how seriously I took my responsibilities as "the accountable manager" in terms of our licence. We got a response. It was a firm "yes".

Now we could get on with the next phase of getting the pre-packaged deal with creditors and investors, the "Scheme of Arrangement" approved by the Irish High Court. We would also have to seek approval in the UK courts, as Cityjet also traded in that jurisdiction and many of our creditors were domiciled there. This was going to be the tricky bit, as the legislation was different. Our lawyers were going to earn their fees on this one as they worked with the examiner to prepare the application for the UK courts. The one creditor I feared would try to block everything was the UK agent of the Portuguese airline with whom we had the major outstanding problem over the cancelled charter series. I was right to worry but the competence of the legal team and the examiner counted for a lot and the threat was outflanked.

We chose a Friday, 6 December, as the day we would go public on the examinership. We would go into the High Court in Dublin that morning and simultaneously our UK lawyers would do likewise in London. The examiner, John McStay, would present his "Scheme of Arrangement" to the judge along with evidence of sufficient funds being available to the company to allow it discharge its ongoing charges for services supplied by third parties during the period of examinership. The hearing was relatively swift and the judge granted us the protection of the court against creditors as he approved the "Scheme of Arrangement", with a review to be heard in January.

Back at the office, I convened a meeting of all managers in my room. I stood before them and told them we were now under examinership and were protected against actions by creditors for the foreseeable future. The important news I had for them was the new investors and that we were assured of a future, but the next few weeks would be difficult as we would be under the glare of the media who would be hunting for any sensational revelations or angles they could find. They were shocked and upset, but they took it well. I promised we would conduct meetings throughout the next day, Saturday, at the Conrad Hotel for all staff and that *all* questions would be answered truthfully.

And then the media bombardment started, with a telephone call from RTÉ radio who wanted a live interview on the one o'clock news magazine programme. Sean O'Rourke was a thoughtful interviewer but the news itself was pretty hard stuff and it wasn't easy being faced with very direct questions and knowing that a lot of people out there are listening to your every word.

The pace never dropped for the rest of the afternoon. I had arranged with Paul White, my good friend and PR adviser, to do interviews with each of the main newspapers at his office. I did five interviews on the trot and then there was RTÉ TV for the six o'clock news. The questioning was tough. "How did a small company like Cityjet amass such losses?" "Where did it all go wrong?" "What about the jobs, are they safe?" We had decided to take a very straight line and also to get everything out on the table now. We strategised that it would be better to empty the cupboard up-front rather than leave it to some energetic investigative journalist to discover something "sensational" and "new" in a few weeks' time. We didn't need an incremental series of bad news; we wanted a positive and heroic recovery story over the next few weeks. So if an interviewer hadn't, in our view, asked strong enough questions, we would prompt him and I would volunteer information. There is no easy way, I reasoned, to say £13 million in accumulated losses in three years, so embrace it and say it loud. I was determined not to shirk any of the hard issues but to be forthright and unapologetic for being in our hour of difficulty.

We had been competing and growing in a ferociously difficult market. We had racked up serious losses, but we were still flying more people and earning more revenue. We had not stood still as we had continued to strive to get to that point of critical mass where we could make financial sense out of our fixed overheads. We had, however, run out of cash to fuel the closing of the gap to the required level of flying activity. We had found new investors who believed we had a future. Yes, it involved support from our creditors, who also took the view that they would trade past losses on forgiving us debt with strong future revenues from continuing to supply an expanding Cityjet. This was pre-Celtic Tiger Ireland. There was still a hang-up over the "f" word — failure. In the US, many businesspeople were not considered successful unless they had a record of previous failures behind them. There was a stigma waiting to be attached to anyone in Ireland who was running a "failing business". Well, I was determined to make sure people understood that examinership, which was still in its infancy as a recently introduced piece of legislation, was an immensely sensible tool of corporate re-construction for a long-term viable business which would otherwise bite the dust due to cash starvation. I was emphatic in my press interviews of our success in forming a coalition between investors and creditors, who all had far more to gain from the company re-emerging out of examinership than it not doing so. Of course, it involved some pain but we were all adults and that was what everybody signed up to, including the existing shareholders and myself. And there were 400 jobs to be protected and we were not going to drop even one member of our tremendously committed crew. We were going forward and we would grow the airline. If I were to paraphrase the thrust and tone of what I was trying to convey on that day of over-exposure, it would be something like this: *So pick over our bones today and we will sit here and tell you everything you think your readers want to know. But tomorrow it's business as usual and we want the support of everybody who believes in honest endeavour and in people who are prepared to have a go to create a new business. That's what the Irish economy needs and we are up for doing it.*

I went to an early Christmas drinks party in a neighbours' house that evening. I was completely shattered and numb. I was beginning to feel a new kind of pressure brought about by the ever-present question: *what if you don't come out of examinership?*

It was an early start on Saturday morning. We had put together a specialist team to manage our way through the media glare over the coming weeks as we worked our way through examinership and managed the business in as normal a fashion as was possible in spite of the heightened visibility. Paul White had been our external adviser on media management and, to his

credit, he brought in Martin Larkin, an experienced PR practitio-
ner, to augment the effort. Luke Mooney and myself rounded off
the four-man panel that would meet practically every single day
at 8.00 am for the next six weeks, although we did give ourselves
a few days off over Christmas (only because journalists do too).
We were determined to avoid death by a thousand cuts in the
media and so our strategy of volunteering all of the bad news up-
front looked like it was pretty much on track. A very good start,
but we would have to remain agile to stay ahead of the probing as
we plotted our way through this period. We also had to be careful
that the kind of press we got did not prove off-putting to regular
passengers who might be tempted to find alternate carriers "until
Cityjet sorted itself out".

Facing the media was one thing, but facing the staff who had
contributed so much in sweat and tears to get the airline this far
was going to be a lot more traumatic. We had meetings all that
afternoon in the Conrad. Basically, we set it up by department
and I outlined exactly where the company was in relation to the
examinership and how it was based on solid commitments from
our creditors — the ones who could choose to close us down by
refusing to supply us — and the new investors who were providing us with the cash to stay in the air for the duration of the examinership and to put in £4 million to drive the reborn business
forward. And there were questions, plenty of them. They were
very straight from the heart, mostly because these people I had
worked so closely with wanted the real story and reassurance that
they would still have a job on the other side of Christmas. But
they also needed to know that their efforts to date weren't about
to go up in smoke. I made sure that each and every one of them
knew that I wasn't going to let the story end here, that we would
get through, that the airline had a future and so did they. At a
break in proceedings that afternoon — not that I needed remind-
ing of the shark-infested waters we were swimming in — but I got
a call on my mobile from the CEO of a prominent regional airline

who thought he would offer "help" in the form of taking over any of our operations in our time of difficulty. I was glad of the call, because it served to heighten my determination to show any blood-sport speculative spectators what Cityjet was made of. We would survive.

We went on the offensive in our marketing. I went into the studio and cut a few radio ads which were very plainly a blatant call for support from the travelling public. The response we got was fantastic. Now our market knew that being in examinership didn't mean liquidation and that we were open and waiting for their business.

There was a lot of logistical planning to be done with the Swedes. They had agreed to loan us an aircraft, which brought our fleet up to five units. Part of the deal was no lease payments for quite a few months. This enabled us to underpin the integrity of our schedule on Dublin/London City and Paris/London City for Air France, while continuing with Dublin/Brussels.

It was also time to pay our compliments to Aer Lingus management. I concluded negotiations with Air UK on a code share agreement on Dublin/London and told Aer Lingus we were discontinuing with the code share with them at the end of the term in March. They were furious. We were delighted. An attempt was made by a senior Aer Lingus executive to try to persuade Air UK to back off the deal with Cityjet. He was wasting his time. It was, however, an interesting insight into the psyche of the national airline. Firstly, they had laughed at our arrival on the scene, flying to a quirky airport called London City. Next they had wooed us at a time when we had threatened EU commission action on the Brussels route. Ultimately, they affirmed their intention not to invest in Cityjet and actually admitted it would suit their purpose if we rolled over and died. But when that didn't happen they became indignant at us having the temerity to fire them out of the code share deal on London City. Strange behaviour. Personally I was very disappointed at what happened, or more to the point what actually didn't happen. No matter, I am still a fan of their front-line staff because they come across to me, a regular passenger, as very real people who practise good customer care in a way that says they genuinely mean it as individuals. In today's competitive world, I think that is priceless. In the relentless push by the current management team at Aer Lingus to emulate Ryanair in the low-fares approach, I really hope they don't copy their rivals too closely by squeezing out what's most precious of all: that "can do" and "want to do" attitude towards the passengers.

It was a busy pre-Christmas run-in. Hans Kallenius was keen on early integration between the respective staff complements of the two airlines and came up with the idea of getting a representative group of people from Cityjet to hop on the evening flight to Malmo from London City and attend a dinner with our new Swedish colleagues. The occasion was the feast of Santa Lucia. We arose very early next morning after four hours of sleep to be whisked to the maintenance hangar at Stirrup Airport, outside Malmo, where we were treated to an intimate and moving ceremony to mark the dawn of the Santa Lucia day of celebration. By 9.00 we were airborne for London City to connect with our mid-morning service back to Dublin. We had forged a real bridge with our new partners in every sense of the word. Hans was a clever man when it came to communication between people. Sadly, it would turn out to be disastrously inconsistent.

Meanwhile, I had to keep Air France happy, not just with the process of a restructuring of the airline that was dependant on the co-operation of creditors. I also had to make them comfortable about the intentions of our new shareholders and especially Malmo Aviation. Paris was visited with purpose.

In the middle of all the hectic activity, maintaining normality and gearing up for the new incarnation of Cityjet with our Swedish partners, there was yet another "Airline of the Year" Awards gig, which we duly attended, putting on our bravest face. I stood behind the microphone, most certainly the first CEO of an airline in examinership to accept yet another award for "Best Airline on Dublin/London". Speculation on our imminent demise had been greatly exaggerated.

It was Christmas and in Cityjet terms that demanded a party. This year, though, it was going to be special. Black tie and the Royal Hospital Kilmainham was a suitable venue for celebrating the commitment of these extraordinary people who had earned their future with this airline. We had made it through to the end of our third year of operations and our chances of making it had gone dramatically up.

Chapter Thirteen

THE VIKING EXPERIENCE

Having gone into the Christmas break with John McStay, the Examiner, presenting the "Scheme of Arrangement" to the High Court on 23 December, creditors had until 6 January to give their answer at a formal creditors' meeting. That day came around quickly and the air of expectation was heavy as we went to meet our fate. John McStay was a skilled facilitator and the response we got from creditors was a unanimous "yes", except for the Revenue Commissioners. We had to wait until 13 January before they would remove their objections to the rescue plan. One week later, the High Court formally approved the "Scheme of Arrangement" and the shortest examinership in the history of the state was lifted. The safety car left the track and normal racing resumed.

The new investment in the company was £4 million but after all of the costs associated with the examinership, the principal one being the payments to creditors, the net new cash we got sight of to develop the business was only £1 million. Granted we had lightened our debt burden by the write-off of £6 million but we still were expected by our shareholders to operate and grow on the equivalent to one week's cost of running the airline. For an airline that was still losing £75,000 a week, this was even more difficult. The rationale behind the tight money was that the investors did not wish to make too much available lest it be gobbled up by creditors on old debt under the "Scheme of Arrangement". The net effect for

the management team and myself meant very little in the tank to
propel ourselves out of the danger zone and into profitability.

However, this was the deal and it was a million times better
than winding up the airline. So we counted the five loaves and two
fishes a few times and when we were sure exactly what we had to
work with we set about building a plan for growing our way out
of trouble. For a very good start we had a fifth aircraft, courtesy of
Malmo, which meant an asset that if sweated could generate revenue for us. We also had an airline partner longer on experience
than us with the same aircraft type, and twice as many of them as
we had. Both airlines had their own respective route networks and
had in common flights into London City. Over the next few weeks
we had a path beaten between Malmo and Dublin as the respective
management teams engaged with each other to make sense out of
every possible synergy we could find. Malmo, while taking a
forty-three per cent stake in Cityjet, had also secured an option to
buy out the Irish shareholders at a future date. The owners of
Malmo were, as I have said previously, vastly wealthy. A cash-
strapped Cityjet could suit their purpose and this was one of my
worries on behalf of the Irish shareholders. The prospect of ultimately selling cheaply if we didn't get the airline over the profit
line quickly loomed large on my radar screen.

However, the collective will to make positive things happen
certainly seemed to be there as we worked well together to devise
a strategy that would translate quickly into a dramatic uplift in
our revenues. We canned the chronically loss-making Dublin/
Brussels route and went for broke on Dublin/London City. We
immediately boosted frequency from five times per business day
to six times, with a commitment to increase this to seven times
daily from March. Aer Lingus were irritated beyond belief and
they let us know. We knew we were on the right track. To give the
dramatic increase in capacity (of some forty per cent) a chance to
take root with the market we introduced a host of deep discounts
and special corporate deals to encourage trial. Our engineering

department benefited enormously from the Malmo experience and superior clout with vendors. Our dispatch reliability in terms of flights leaving on time went way up. Within three months, the gamble was to pay off as the forty per cent increase in capacity was to deliver a sixty-six per cent increase in revenues. The replacement code share deal with Air UK was going really well and they were selling strongly on our behalf in the UK market. Our marketing campaign was running on high octane. I organised numerous media interviews and made public speaking appearances wherever I could get in front of a strong corporate audience. The storyline was simple. This was the little airline that refused to be beaten. We had escaped death and were fighting back against those who had prematurely written our obituary. We were in the business of flying people and we were committed to delivering what we always strived to deliver, a customer-driven service. I engineered a second appearance on *The Late Late Show* with a strong story to tell.

The afternoon before, I travelled north once again for a late evening meeting in Malmo and a further one the next morning. I rode in the helicopter on the downtown scheduled service from Malmo across a most inhospitable-looking stretch of water as we crossed over to Copenhagen Airport to get an early afternoon flight to Dublin. I reflected on the interview I was going to have with Gay Byrne on live TV in a matter of hours. I was exhausted, but not just from the past twenty-four hours of travelling and meeting late into the night; I was also carrying a much deeper tiredness that had been building up for the past four years. If people really knew what the pressure was like, what would they think? "Poor guy" or "poor fool"?! I came to the rapid conclusion that people don't care that much about the personal wear-and-tear behind tough business stories. People like winners and winners don't moan. So tonight would be another success story, provided I could steer Gaybo away from too many searching questions about how dark my world had got during the twelve months since I had last been on the show brimming with a wistful naivety about how we were set to do great things with our little airline.

The interview went well and the effect it had on our marketing programme was probably best measured in the strong progress in bookings in the weeks that followed. We stepped up the radio ads and the media interviews as we watched the load factor on every flight climb. It was working. Maybe it was part sympathy vote, part admiration for our tenacity in hanging in there or just that what we had to offer made sense. I'm sure it was possibly all of this. But it certainly was working.

Over the next few weeks there was an intense focus on how we might put the two airlines together in an operational sense and develop a combined stronger route network. Malmo had made a virtue out of flying into Stockholm's Bromma Airport which is situated right downtown. Just like London City Airport, Bromma could not take anything bigger than the BAe 146, so the competitive edge Malmo had against SAS was very pronounced. Their big rival had to operate into Stockholm's international airport, some forty kilometres outside of the city. Malmo Aviation served the business communities of Gotenberg, Malmo and Stockholm and all of their flights were skewed towards providing capacity in the early morning and evening. They didn't bother flying in the off-peak times as they didn't need to. They enjoyed "stuffed to the brim" aircraft in the peaks with passengers paying premium prices. The aircraft were not utilised more than four hours a day and had most weekends off. Compared to the Cityjet fleet, the Malmo aircraft did less than half the amount of flying. And in summer, there was a six-week period where two-thirds of the fleet stayed on the ground as the business community took their summer holidays. To us, this business model defied conventional common sense, yet it made a healthy margin.

The big downside Malmo had, however, was the over-protective nature of the unions who had to be consulted on each and every potential variation to existing work practices. Added to this was the very high cost of employment in Sweden due to the penal rates of social insurance, approximating to forty-eight per cent of gross salary on top. In complete contrast, Cityjet was non-unionised and rates of pay were considerably lower especially with a comparative social insurance cost of twelve per cent. We put in a lot of work to develop a model that would see a combined fleet of thirteen aircraft and crews interchanging in the operation of an efficient route network. To be fully effective and to really extract the cost savings, it would be ideal to operate off one licence, either the Irish one or the Swedish one. No matter which way we would go on this, there was a well-founded fear that the Swedish unions were going to create obstacles to such a merged operation. So the words "integration" and "merger" dropped out of the vocabulary as we resolved to optimise every other form of synergy, stopping short of banging the two airlines into one.

Meanwhile we were continuing to deepen our relationship with Air France. They were happy with our performance on the Paris/London City service, which was now, next to Concorde, producing the highest passenger revenue per kilometre yield in the entire Air France global network. It was all business class and passengers were paying stg£330 per return journey for their fifty-minute experience. Talks on launching a Dublin/Paris service were at an advanced stage, with Air France agreeing to stand down their once-daily Airbus A320 service on the route in favour of Cityjet operating a twice-daily service with a BAe 146. Air France were also prepared to buy a significant number of seats under a code share deal and to market the service through their established distribution system worldwide.

In the background, the Irish and Swedish board members seemed to be making good headway in the trust-building stakes. In mid-March of that year (1997) the Irish directors were invited to Stockholm to present the new business model for Cityjet to the full board of Malmo Aviation. If there were any cracks beginning to form in this marriage, they were still very well concealed.

Exactly a month later, we celebrated the opening of Cityjet's new offices in the atrium in the terminal building at Dublin Airport. The Swedes were there in force to meet with Alan Dukes TD, the Minister for Transport, as he cut the ribbon. We retired to Roly's Bistro later that evening where we played host to the Wiklund brothers and Hans Kallenius. All was well, I thought. Just two days later, I was to get my first glimpse of the origins of the forthcoming Swedish power play.

Hans had called a special meeting of the "Integration Committee" drawn from the respective senior teams of the two airlines. The plan was to meet at London City on Friday. Hans and I would then travel to Goodwood that evening where we were due to be entertained for the weekend by BAe along with all other CEOs of 146 operators. The meeting had nothing to do with integration. We were ambushed by Hans and his finance director, who launched a blistering attack on our trading figures. This was quite irrational, especially as we had made such incredible progress on driving revenues up. No, we hadn't broken into profit yet but we had seriously reduced our rate of losses while dramatically increasing the scope of operations. Hans's performance was tantrum-like and bordering on being personally offensive at times to different members of our team. I was surprised and annoyed. Jane and Hans's wife, Ann-Margaret, arrived separately later that afternoon at London City and the four of us headed off into rush-hour traffic for a two-and-a-half-hour drive to Goodwood. I didn't speak to Hans for the whole trip and I was still fuming over what had happened at the meeting. It was deeply frustrating, especially as Jane and I could not have a meaningful conversation with him in the car and I was in no mood for small talk involving all of us as a quartet. The game seemed to be about to change but I still had no real idea how much and how fast it was going to change.

The marketing campaign steamed on with the launch of our own frequent flyer programme which, as our promotion copy had it, was *"simply city or in a word simplycity"*. Our Whisper Club for

PAs and other frequent bookers of their managers on Cityjet was in full swing. The next big increment in the story was the May Day launch of the Dublin/Paris service, which the media covered extensively. Meanwhile Hans seemed to be getting back to the style I had been accustomed to and was once again affable and charming to all around him. He came to Dublin on his way to a long weekend in Connemara with his wife, his two grown-up children and their partners. He had specifically asked us to organise his itinerary to capture the essence of old Ireland. We laid it on with an authentic experience of Irish storytelling, poetry and music by peat fires. Good places to stay and excellent food. We could do nothing about the rain, which never stopped, apparently.

Barely more than a week later, Paul Coulson and myself travelled to Paris to meet a fellow Irishman in the person of John Power, who had recently joined Air France from his former position as President of British Airways (North America) and now occupied the number three slot in terms of overall seniority. The purpose of the meeting was to seek an assurance on a promise by Air France to allow us increase our frequency on our new Dublin/Paris service to three times a day and also to review the price they were paying for seats under the code share arrangement. It wasn't the best of times to have this kind of meeting — it was day one of a four-day stoppage by Air France pilots. We had arranged for Hans and Stefan Wiklund to be at the meeting also. John Power was impressive and he was accompanied by Bruno Matheu with whom I had been developing a good working relationship over previous months and who would become crucial to the wellbeing of Cityjet into the future. With the niceties dispensed with, Hans went on an astonishingly confrontational attack on our hosts. He accused them of taking advantage of Cityjet in pricing and of condemning us to a form of bondage. Paul and I looked in horror at each other as we could scarcely believe what we were witnessing. It was brutal.

John Power drew on all of his professional experience to respond without letting his emotions lead. His message was a simple one and quite Irish. "People should not come into our house and treat us in this way" was his opening line, delivered in a calm tone of voice. I was horrified and quite baffled. Without an instant damage assessment, I wasn't sure how close this man sitting beside me had just come to destroying the relationship I had spent two-and-a-half years building up. Paul Coulson was visibly stunned but he moved rapidly to dilute the stinging effect of Hans's outburst. Paul tried to reassure Air France that he was quite sure Hans did not mean exactly what he had said and that the commercial connection Cityjet enjoyed with the French carrier was of enormous importance to us. As far as trying to go after the objectives we had for the meeting, it was now clearly a lost cause and damage limitation became the new priority.

Paul Coulson and I did our best to beat a dignified retreat on the day and went for a meal with Hans and Stefan to sift through the wreckage of what had gone on at this strangest of meetings with arguably our most important ally for attaining a balanced growth. The charm had returned to Hans's interactions with us but it was very clear he was of a different disposition to us when it came to having an appetite for moving forward with the French. We reminded both Hans and Stefan that developing the relationship with Air France was an important plank in our agreed strategy for growth for Cityjet, as the lower-risk profile of contract flying and franchised routes was the perfect counterbalance to developing our "own risk" routes. We got a sort of a muffled response which bordered on "maybe you're right" with a bit of "we'll be more diplomatic in the future". We had been warned of things to come but we didn't attach enough significance to what we had just witnessed that afternoon in Paris. In the meantime, I knew it was going to be my job to smooth and square things with the French in the weeks ahead.

Chapter Fourteen

IT MIGHT HAVE BEEN BETTER IF WE
HAD EATEN THE FATTED PIG

A s ever, I was acutely conscious of our very tight cash position and I began to focus on some contingency planning to
raise more money. The four aircraft we had on lease from US Air
had given us horrific maintenance difficulties. We were concerned
particularly about specific modifications which had been logged
in the records as having being carried out during the US$2 million
overhaul carried out on each aircraft taken out of desert storage
and which we now suspected might not have been actually done
to the required standard in every case. This had resulted in us in-
curring considerable cost in inspecting and putting this right
combined with the added expense of aircraft downtime and the
consequent hiring in from other operators.

We let US Air know what we knew and invited a meeting of
minds around how we might arrive at a sensible resolution. A key
thing we went after was the value US Air had in their books for
the aircraft. To our immense relief, this turned out to be an average of US$6 million per aircraft. I commissioned an independent
detailed survey of each aircraft from the market leaders in used
aircraft valuation. The answer we got back was an average value
of US$8 million per aircraft. I formed a think tank along with my
two very financially astute Cityjet colleagues, Aidan Keane and
Hugh Rodgers, to come up with a formula for translating this

"gap" in valuation into cash for the airline. It would take a bit of time for us to come up with the answer but we would stay on the trail over the next few weeks because we could sense a way home.

We continued with our energetic marketing campaign, covering direct visits to corporates and travel agents. Our radio and press advertising rumbled on. In addition to being constantly in communication with Malmo Aviation and Paul Coulson, our Chairman, I also put a lot of time into keeping individual Irish shareholders informed about what was happening. I had succeeded in repairing the fences for the time being with Air France after the Viking outburst in mid-May in Paris. I thought we were in good shape for the board meeting of 3 July as we had worked especially hard on the latest iteration of the forward business plan. I was unusually relaxed ahead of this meeting because there had been an immense amount of close collaborative preparatory work between the financial departments of Malmo and Cityjet.

I don't think the meeting was even thirty minutes old when the bomb went off. There was a mistake in the calculation of the forward cost of fuel and it was £0.8 million the wrong way. Yes, it was an error, a flaw in an Excel formula. Of course it wasn't good enough, but how the Swedes, aggressively led by Hans, seized the moment to press home maximum advantage! *They were outraged! This was a disaster! The airline's future was precarious enough without another hole of this magnitude in the projections!* The Irish directors representing shareholders were painted into a corner. Hans picked up on their anxiety and called time out. The huddle began with Hans shuttling between the two camps posturing as the broker of *"the best way out of jail"* for everyone. I could see the worst fears of the Irish shareholders in their eyes as they began to accept that the only way out of this might be to cede control to the Swedes, who would take on the liabilities of the business but pay little or nothing to shareholders for the privilege.

I was disgusted at the ease with which Hans had railroaded the Irish shareholders but it was clear I wasn't going to be listened to, not today. I accompanied the Swedish team down to the boarding gate for their flight to Copenhagen. We had time in hand and so I suggested we get a pint of Guinness and some smoked salmon in the bar at the B gates in Dublin Airport. I wanted to see if they would let their slip show even a little as they relaxed ahead of their flight home. They were in good spirits and were conversing in Swedish among themselves. I didn't need to have a command of their native language to recognise Hans and Stefan in celebratory mode, having "putting one over" on the Irish. I was furious but I was not going to let them know that. I needed to think this one through carefully.

The events of the board meeting on Thursday dominated my thinking as I headed into the weekend. I had promised my daughter Sarah that I would bring her to the air show in Baldonnell aerodrome, just outside of Dublin, on Sunday. We went early in the morning and spent time working our way around many of the static displays and meeting with a number of my good acquaintances in the Irish Air Corps, who were our hosts for the day. I was completely distracted. My nervous system was about to explode. I could not contain my sense of anger at the opportunistic move I had witnessed two days previously. I could contain myself no longer. I phoned Paul Coulson at home on this beautiful Sunday morning. As soon as I started to talk, I found myself competing with, of all the aircraft in the world, a Swedish Saab Viggen fighter jet doing a deafening practice run directly overhead. (I wasn't to know that the very same aircraft manufacturer would be the source of much grief for us in the not too distant future.)

Anyway, I got my point across to Paul in spite of the deafening background noise. I relayed the image of what I had witnessed at the boarding gate on Thursday. I told him I was certain the Swedes had seized their chance to stiff the Irish shareholders and I expressed my profound frustration at the lack of fight against this opportunistic push. He responded well. He left me in no doubt that he was not going to be rolled over. I enjoyed the

rest of the air show with Sarah. Monday would be the start of another series of steps to head off predators at the pass.

I was not against a merged airline; in fact I had put in a lot of
effort over the previous months to try to make sense out of an
enlarged route network that leveraged the respective operational
resources of the two airlines. I had come to see real potential in
working closely with most of the Malmo senior management and
I personally subscribed to the ambition of a pragmatic joint operation. However, I had developed what I believed to be well-
grounded misgivings about Hans's leadership style.

Paul Coulson got his act together and let it be known that the
majority shareholding in Cityjet was not about to be given away.
We were invited to hold a meeting of directors in Sweden at
Stefan Wiklund's family summer retreat. We arrived late at night
after a long drive from Stirrup Airport, outside Malmo. The house
and grounds set deep in the countryside were impressive.

Following a great breakfast, we adjourned to a pavilion in the
extensive gardens for our meeting. It was tough going to get to a
point of convergence. We broke up into two distinct groups, with
the Swedes retiring to another chalet-type building in the garden.
Hans and I kept up a shuttle service, symbolically meeting in the
middle of the ground between the two buildings to exchange the
latest positions/responses from the respective camps. It was farci-
cal, but it was happening. We eventually all came together again
and a deal was struck. There would be a proportionate injection of
additional funds from shareholders to shore up the hole in the
figures caused by the fuel miscalculation and we would continue
with no change in the respective equity holdings. The handshakes
were firm.

However, a fatal error of judgement was about to be made by
the Irish contingent. Stefan and his family wanted us to stay that
night to celebrate a particular festive summer occasion. He had
especially brought in a wild boar and he wished to host a lavish
banquet for his guests. Paul Coulson, Brendan McDonald and

Brendan Dowling had been agitated at the drawn-out proceedings of the day and were anxious to get home. They were also still quite infuriated at Hans and Stefan, even though a way forward had been agreed. The last thing they wanted to do was to sit and sup wine and eat pig with these people who had wrecked their heads. They said "no thanks". Something inside me told me this wasn't a good decision.

The message came through the next day in a phone call from Stefan to Paul Coulson. Stefan had changed his mind and all bets were off. No deal. It was a very expensive dinner to have missed. Stalemate.

I was bursting for a few days away, so I organised a five-day trip to Malmo and Stockholm for Jane and her son Michael together with my girls Sarah and Eleanor. Our son, Ross, who was only two years old, stayed behind with family. The weather was incredible and we had a fantastic time, especially in Stockholm. We came back to Malmo and I went to meet Hans, Stefan and the management team in the airline. Hans was really keen for me to represent a revised position to Paul Coulson and the others and at one stage hinted at there being a good future in the enlarged entity going forward if I could sell their deal. I made it clear that as CEO I was working for the Board of Directors in the interests of all shareholders. By this stage, the trust had gone between the Swedes and the Irish shareholders and there was little appetite in Dublin for trying once more. We would, however, get to a resolution within weeks and the foundation for it lay in unlocking the trapped value in the aircraft from US Air.

The Irish shareholders were not up for putting more capital into the airline and they were fearful of the likely prospect of losing Malmo as an airline partner. They also recognised that Stefan Wiklund was reluctant to spend any more money on airlines and that his "volte-face" on the deal in the garden shed was probably more to do with his reticence to invest further than on the Irish turning down the pig supper. But who knows?

I propositioned the Irish shareholders. What if their investment in the airline was secured against the "metal" of the aircraft?
We had cracked how to unlock the value in the planes. I took a
shelf company and configured it to be a special-purpose leasing
vehicle under the name of Janesville Limited. I went to Anglo
Irish Bank and asked them how much they would lend to Janesville to fund the purchase, from US Air, of two aircraft valued at
US$8 million each plus three spare engines valued at just under
US$0.75 million a piece. I intimated that there would be strong
shareholder support from the key Irish stakeholders in Cityjet in
terms of injecting capital into Janesville. I then went to Yeoman,
Paul Coulson's investment company, and to each of the other
Irish shareholders to seek commitments in principle to funding
the aircraft and engines purchased on the basis that the Bank was
prepared to lend in the region of US$10 million on the deal. Next,
I had to get US Air to play ball. I had been talking to them for
weeks to get them into condition for the specific type of transac-
tion that was needed here. They would be happy to be paid
US$6 million per plane and US$0.75 million per spare engine. I
had a credible market valuation of US$8 million per aircraft.

The Bank and the Cityjet shareholders would be happy to put
up a total of US$18.5 million, via Janesville, on the basis that the
aircraft and engines would be leased from Janesville to Cityjet on
a seven-year term and at full market rates. I needed US Air to
make a special payment back to Cityjet in the amount of
US$4 million and for this to be categorised as a compensatory
payment for the shortcomings in the maintenance condition of the
two aircraft on delivery to Cityjet. In this way, Cityjet was getting
the benefit of additional funding of US$4 million, which of course
was coming indirectly from the Irish shareholders. However, instead of them injecting this capital into Cityjet, which action
would carry with it a very high risk, as it would not be secured
against any assets, they now had their investment secured on the
aircraft and engines which Cityjet were leasing from their leasing

company. Should anything happen Cityjet, the shareholders could re-possess the assets of the two aircraft and three spare engines and avoid being in the back of the queue behind creditors. It was brilliantly simple and they went for it — not all of them but the Bank of course plus Yeoman, Brendan McDonald, Mike Murphy and one of our institutional investors.

Now we had the juice to face up to the Swedes' reticence to put more money into Cityjet. We could solve their two problems of withdrawing without financial loss and, almost as important for them, without loss of face. We replicated our deal with Janesville on their behalf. We centred the deal on a third aircraft from US Air, which was in service with Cityjet. We encouraged Stefan Wiklund to construct his own Janesville and to obtain a loan from a Swedish bank of his choosing. He agreed to allow us lease the aircraft for eighteen months, at which point we would have the option of purchasing it from him or relinquishing our right to a continued lease. In this way we unlocked value for Wiklund which compensated him for the Irish investors paying no money to him for the transfer of his shares in Cityjet to them. We could have kept this deal on a third 146 for Janesville which would have provided more cash to Cityjet but we deemed it better to forfeit this opportunity and use it to indirectly finance the getting rid of the Swedes at no cost to the Irish shareholders.

So the Swedes transferred their forty-three per cent shareholding to the Irish investors in return for the aircraft deal we constructed for them. We went public on the combined deal a week before Christmas and, with clever media spinning, we eclipsed the departure of the Swedes with the stronger story of Cityjet buying two jets barely more than ten months since emerging from examinership.

Meanwhile our relationship with Air France was very much back in the groove, with no lasting effects from the extraordinary confrontation with the Swedes back in May. I had kept Bruno Matheu of Air France informed about the impending departure of

Malmo Aviation as shareholders and he didn't seem to see too many negatives in that development. We were asked to establish a route from Strasbourg to London City for Air France, to be operational by the end of October. We said "yes" and we met the deadline. We were now stretched to the limit in terms of our small fleet. We needed more aircraft but we were now for the first time caught in a period which saw a shortage in BAe 146 availability, so successful had BAe and US Air been in moving their surplus aircraft. Through our very well-established network of contacts in the world of the BAe 146 we had always maintained excellent intelligence on every unit that might become available worldwide. But this was a drought. To compound our problem, Malmo Aviation wanted us to return the aircraft we had been leasing from them since the previous December. It looked like we would be going down to four 146s instead of expanding up to six units. There were aircraft due back off lease from other operators some twelve to eighteen months out, but that was no use to us. There were also a number of aircraft in service with the well-funded Debonair whose business model seemed decidedly shaky but it looked to us that it would take another year before they would run out of bank notes to set fire to.

We were getting desperate, as we could see no way of getting our hands on more aircraft quickly. Then the unthinkable began to come into focus. What about another aircraft type? Crossair, who had been the pace-setters for regional airlines in Europe for years, had apparent success with operating the BAe Avro RJ (same as the 146 with smarter avionics and slightly modernised versions of the same bad engine) in parallel with the Saab 2000. The Saab 2000 was a very high-performance turboprop with fifty seats and a cruising speed only marginally below that of the 146. In fact, its superior rate of climb and operational service ceiling meant it could practically match journey times of the 146 on flights of an hour's duration or less. By the end of October, we had commenced dialogue with Saab. We immersed ourselves in the technical performance details of the aircraft type. There were only sixty-two Saab 2000s in existence, all having been built in 1994 and 1995. Crossair, as the launch customer, accounted for almost half of the entire production. SAS, in a show of patriotic fervour, had taken ten units, while Regional Airlines based in Nantes were operating a fleet of eleven. Outside of these concentrations of sizeable fleets there were a few units with Deutsche BA, one somewhere in the Asian Pacific rim and, amazingly, three with General Motors in the US, who were operating them as corporate executive shuttles.

There had been great hopes for the Saab 2000, as Saab had enjoyed huge commercial success with the thirty-four-seat S-340, especially in the US. The Saab 2000 was conceived as the answer to the lack of a high-speed, high-altitude fifty-seater in the regional market. The delay in rolling units off the production line — rumoured to be a result of entertaining too many late changes to specification demanded by launch customer, Crossair — had been costly. Bombardier were already offering their fifty-seat jet, the CRJ, and Embraer were about to flood the market with their EMB 145 fifty-seat jet. Embraer were exploiting their Brazilian government-backed credit export scheme, which effectively meant customer airlines could buy a unit for under US$14 million compared to US$18 million plus for the Bombardier CRJ. Bombardier's legal challenge to this scheme would eventually be upheld, but not before Embraer had succeeded in moving some three hundred or more aircraft. With a sticker price at the time of US$14 million for a brand new Saab 2000, "almost as fast as a jet turboprop", it is easy to see why the production line was closed almost as soon as it had started. No matter; on paper, the Saab 2000 was a seriously good aircraft. Besides, it also had the short-field performance which was essential for operations at London City. The Bombardier and Embraer jet equivalents hadn't got this capability. So, in the absence of any near-term availability of more BAe 146s, we had little option but to get our heads into the bucket and see if we could make sense of it.

Chapter Fifteen

COME INTO MY PARLOUR, SAID SAAB

The speed of transition from speculative discussion to hard negotiation with Saab Aircraft's leasing arm was incredible. This was early December and we were talking about their capacity to provide us with two aircraft, the first by March, the second no later than a month behind that. I was all too aware of the nightmare scenario of a small airline operating two distinctly different aircraft types. The restrictions in terms of pilots only being permitted by the regulatory authority to be current on one aircraft type placed a big cost burden on us, not to mention the inflexibility of this set-up. The holding of an entirely separate and distinctly different inventory of spare parts and the requirement for engineers licensed for this specific aircraft type was both a financial and operational headache.

To add to our challenge, we had learned of the acute shortage of engines from Allison, who were in the process of being taken over by Rolls Royce. The emerging information on the reliability performance of this engine induced a strong sense of *déjà vu* as we came to realise that lightning can and, as we would find out, does strike twice. We had grown accustomed to the shortcomings of the 502 engine on the BAe 146; could we handle the dubious performance of the Allison AE 2000 on the Saab?

No matter; we needed more aircraft for the summer season of 1998, commencing in March. We would only have four 146s. Incredibly, there weren't any more out there to be had, other than on

short-term wet lease from third-party operators. Prohibitively expense wet-leasing was not something we relished, as the margin
from passenger revenue was going to the other operator and not
us. We were also facing into considerable downtime in the fleet,
due to the mandatory installation of an "area navigation" system,
known as the R-Nav, which was not fitted as standard in aircraft
manufactured pre-1990 or so. We would be giving enough money
away on the continuous hiring-in of a 146 replacement from another carrier over the three months of January, February and
March, as we rotated our four jets through the retrofit. The R-Nav
fit would take two weeks per aircraft, which is why we had "damp-
leased" in a 146. In a damp lease, as the term might suggest, we
didn't get quite as soaked as in a wet lease. It still meant using the
external operator's aircraft and pilots but with our cabin crew. One
advantage, of course, was that it released some of our 146 drivers
for conversion to the Saab, as there was a good supply of more 146-
qualified pilots, especially in Australia, to replace them when we
had our full fleet restored complete with their R-Nav installations.

At a push, one more aircraft would do but there was no point
in taking just one of type. To get any scale effect in technical support and operations dynamics, we would need at least two Saab
2000s. Having the additional capacity would allow us to boost
frequency dramatically on Dublin/London City as we knew this
was precisely what the regular business passenger wanted. These
additional flights, with fifty-seat aircraft promising a relatively
lower operating costs per seat to the 146, would enable us to focus
our marketing of the increased frequency on the higher yield end
of the market without an increased dependency on the leisure or
VFR ("visiting friends or relatives") segments. But to fully justify
two units, we would have to have enough flying activity, and we
came up with the notion of operating three return services per
week-day from Cork to London City.

Just before the Christmas break, we committed ourselves by
way of paying a deposit to Saab for the delivery of two aircraft, the

first in March and the second in April. Given their immense speed for a turboprop, there was preparatory work to be done to the Saab 2000s to make them capable of landing at London City. They needed a steep approach fit fitted to the avionics suite, which would enable them to shoot an approach at a glide scope angle of 5.2 degrees compared to the conventional and more shallow angle of nose down of 3.6 degrees. The flaps had to be modified and vortex generators fitted to the ailerons. All of this would cost money and it would take time to requisition parts from vendors. Our stretched engineering department would have to monitor the progress of Saab in this work in parallel with the major programme now underway on the 146 fleet to install the R-Nav system.

Our route network for summer 1998 was now looking like Dublin/London City, Dublin/Paris, Paris/London City, with an expectation of Cork/London City. The reality was that we would continue to design the aircraft utilisation repeatedly for many weeks, to come up with the optimum combination of the 146s and Saab 2000s to satisfy passenger demand and produce the best possible economic result. If there were PhDs awarded for this art of tasking aircraft to timetables, then we surely could have been called "the flying doctors"!

Air France were already pushing for us to commit to an expanded programme with them for summer 1999, which was some fifteen months away. It was clear they wanted more 146 capacity from us as they were planning on a high-frequency service on Paris/Florence and the BAe aircraft was the only jet capable of getting in and out of this very challenging Italian airfield. The scale of the proposed operation on Paris/Florence dictated an additional two aircraft by March 1999. The French also wanted us to go up to five return flights per day on the Paris/London City route, which was tricky, as it called for an additional thirty per cent of a 146. How to utilise the other seventy per cent of this additional aircraft would represent both a commercial and a schedule integration challenge. I was gambling on the fact that, as BAe delivered more

RJs, the modernised version of the 146, to their customer airlines, more 146s would be released to the market in time for the following year. We had long since ruled out taking delivery of new RJs ourselves on the grounds of leasing rates of almost US$200,000 per month per aircraft compared to the US$110,000 per month we were paying for our 146s, which did exactly the same job.

Our operation of a 146 on the Strasbourg/London City service for the French was due to terminate in March, as they had decided the loads only justified a fifty-seat aircraft and they planned to place a contract with Regional Airlines for a Saab 2000 operation. However, we were contracted by our old friends in Malmo Aviation to commence a Stockholm/London City service for them from April, the aircraft coming off the Strasbourg route. So the forward thinking was that an increasing fleet of Saab 2000s could handle all our Dublin/London City business and probably Cork/ London. I was confident that Cityjet's lower cost base could result in our winning back the Strasbourg/London City business next year as we would then have a proven capability with the Saab 2000.

The clock was counting down rapidly to the arrival of the Saabs. We renewed our contact with Crossair to learn as much as we could from their experience of operating the type. Their flight operations department provided us with instructor pilots to help accelerate the conversion process. We placed our heavy maintenance contract for the Saabs with Regional Airlines, headquartered in Nantes. Meanwhile, some of our engineers went back to school in Sweden to get up to speed on this high-tech airplane. Our Saab 2000 project team was in high gear with daily review meetings and new actions being taken to keep the critical path to early delivery on track. Normally it takes twelve months or more from decision date to implementation of a new aircraft. When it is a new aircraft type for the airline, then the timelines extend outwards.

We were attempting to do this in four months.

The hyperactivity was feeling awfully familiar. While we were consumed with getting our Saab fleet delivered and operational by the end of March, we were also tying up the deal with Malmo, which meant setting up a crew base in Stockholm to operate their new Stockholm/London City service for them. I had initiated talks with Regional Airlines in Nantes to see how we might co-operate, since we were both flying Saab 2000s and we each had a relationship with Air France. Things moved more quickly with Regional than I could have imagined. They had an acute pilot shortage after taking delivery of a number of new Embraer 145 regional jets. It now seemed probable that they would transfer one of their Saab 2000s to our licence, which we would crew and operate under a sub-contract to their contract with Air France for the Strasbourg/ London City route, which we were due to lose as it had proved too thin on passenger loads for a 146. Suddenly, instead of only having a fleet of two Saabs, we were going to have three. The economies of scale in terms of technical support for our additional aircraft type were improving.

All of this intense effort, where our best people were completely absorbed with trying to do the near-impossible to make sure the airline broke through the pain barrier of critical mass, weighed heavily on me.

I was still trying to deal with the bitter disappointment of the Malmo Aviation saga. On paper, it had been a good pairing. Together we should have been capable of rationalising our respective cost bases through merger and grown quickly to a joint fleet of twenty 146s, with a sensible route network of profitable domestic services in Sweden coupled with Irish and Swedish routes to London City. The Swedes had a wealthy backer in the Crafoord Wiklund family and I was certain the Irish shareholders would have responded in kind to any funding initiative by the Swedes toward expanding the joint operation. But it wasn't to be and for reasons that didn't — and still don't — make any sense to me. You can't always understand it and sometimes there is no understanding in it. It just is as it is and no amount of sweating will change the outcome.

There had to be a better or smarter way to get to profitability faster with the help of the right type of well-funded partner. I was seeking out more new possibilities in this domain. Our relationship with Air UK, which was a wholly owned subsidiary of KLM, was good. The code share we had with them on London City/Dublin was working okay. I upped the tempo in my regular discourse with Henny Essenberg, their CEO. There was interest in exploring a deeper coupling of Air UK with Cityjet and this was being discussed in KLM Head Office in Schipol. We would be invited shortly to strut our stuff.

I was also trying to get something going with Eurowings of Germany, a highly successful regional operator who had an excellent working relationship with both KLM and Air France, at the expense of Lufthansa in both instances. After two days of solid wrangling with the people from Saab over the finer details of the forthcoming delivery of aircraft, I went on the first of my pilgrimages to Nuremburg to see what piece of common ground might support a conversation. The fact that Eurowings were also a BAe 146 operator, alongside their enormous fleet of ATR turboprop aircraft was a good pipe opener. We offered to cover their night-stop 146s at Paris CDG with our engineers, which would save them a lot of money in salaries and allowances. In exchange, we could ask them to handle our reservations and sales at CDG, which would be good for us as we had a very small marketing presence in Paris. And so the dance developed, up to the point of talking about routes between Germany and Ireland. We would have a few more meetings. On the engineering side, there was genuine interest but sadly the commercial challenges Eurowings faced were taxing the minds of their senior management. They were facing a choice between respective ultimatums from both KLM and Air France as to who they would continue to partner exclusively. The prospect of doing something with a small but dynamic Irish outfit didn't really stand out on their radar among the clutter of challenges and opportunities facing them.

Those last days of February and early March 1998 saw me in Malmo, Nuremburg and Nantes, with a couple of days locking horns with Saab somewhere in the middle. Air France were impacting a lot on our time to work on the following year's flying programme and our key shareholders wanted me to brief them on what was going on. The 146 we had hired in damp from Flightline to cover for our R-Nav installation programme had achieved the distinction of being regularly unserviceable since it started on Dublin/Paris for us. Tempers were getting shorter around virtually every department in Cityjet as operations, engineering and commercial were all feeling the pressure. London City Airport were being sticky with Malmo Aviation about giving them slots for the Stockholm/London City service which we would be operating for them. We started into a complicated triangular negotiation which finally got resolved after a lot of angst that could have been avoided.

Out of the blue, our Commercial Director, Peter Ribeiro, came up with the bones of a deal with East Midlands Airport, who were prepared to offer us a substantial package of incentives to operate a Saab 2000 service from Dublin. The potential deal would make the prospect of a Cork/London City service look a far higher risk. We got stuck into the numbers and commissioned a recognised independent route analysis expert to second-guess the traffic projections produced by East Midlands. The figures stood up and the cash contribution from the airport was real. We said "no" to Cork and immediately diverted our efforts into getting the Dublin/East Midlands route up and running. We were sure we could launch within six weeks and we did.

Chapter Sixteen

THINGS MIGHT HAVE GOT BORING

There were rumours of impending strife doing the rounds at Dublin airport. It had been brewing all week and now it was Friday. Michael O'Leary of Ryanair had steadfastly refused over previous weeks to give negotiating rights to SIPTU, the trade union claiming to represent a small minority of baggage handlers working with the rapidly rising airline. O'Leary, as is his style, pushed things to the edge and taunted the union with a provocative banner draped on the outside of the Ryanair head office at Dublin Airport. SIPTU weren't going to stand for that in their own backyard. Dublin Airport was their heartland and their membership was drawn from the staff of Aer Lingus and most other airlines, handling companies, the airport police, fire crews, airport administrative staff, etc. The notable exceptions were Ryanair and Cityjet, whose staff chose not to join the union.

We actually overheard it that Friday afternoon in early March. Adjacent to our offices, a meeting was being conducted by the prominent senior figure in SIPTU in that part of their world. He was addressing airport police officers and fire crew and it was blatant. They were going to force the airport to close the following day, Saturday, in sympathy with the forty baggage handlers in Ryanair whom O'Leary refused to allow SIPTU to represent in wage bargaining.

We geared up for the morning. All managers would report for duty, though quite what sort of duties we weren't really sure. But our objective was clear. Our flights would not be stopped by the unlawful actions of trade union members. The entrances to the airport were manned by Aer Lingus- and Aer Rianta-uniformed members of SIPTU bearing placards. This was secondary picket-ing, as the dispute, if there was one at all, was at Ryanair. Within an hour, it was evident that pickets weren't being passed by other SIPTU members and, incredibly, Aer Lingus and British Midlands shut down operations. As Aer Lingus were the biggest handling agent for visiting airlines, their flights were also stopped. The air-port police walked off the job and were shortly followed by the firemen. The Aer Rianta management put their contingency plan into operation and manned the fire-fighting vehicles. But there were huge holes in security and the airport was now a dangerous, potentially lethal place. There were protesters standing in front of Ryanair aircraft on the ramp to impede their operation. They were removed by airport management personnel. All of Ryanair's flights continued to operate, as did all of Cityjet's. But this was a scary situation, with the terminal building overflowing with agi-tated and frustrated would-be passengers, striking workers and television crews.

Throughout that Saturday and Sunday, the news reporting, especially by RTÉ, was to my ears outrageously biased in favour of SIPTU. I made many attempts to break into live discussions on radio and to speak with the head of news. I left several blunt mes-sages. On that Sunday afternoon, I took a break from the war zone that the airport now resembled to go to watch a schools junior rugby cup match at Donnybrook. My close friend, Barry Cole-man's son, Killian, was playing for Terenure College. My mobile phone buzzed in my pocket during a lull in the noise of commit-ted spectators. It was Aileen O'Meara, a senior reporter with RTÉ. "My boss, the head of news, knows you've been upset about the balance of our coverage of the strife at the airport and he has de-cided to give you some airtime to put your point of view across.

I'm at the roundabout outside the airport to do a live link-up for the TV news at six. Can you be here then?"

Terenure won the match and we went to the Dropping Well for a drink. I left Jane in good company and made my way back out to the airport. It was an intimidating experience, standing at the side of the road in front of the news crew and being heckled aggressively by the picket line. I said my piece. *"No, I'm not on Michael O'Leary's side and I don't think he has handled things too cleverly. But two wrongs don't make a right and what has happened here, with essentially illegal secondary picketing, is unjustifiable. This is madness. There is a travelling public who depend on us in the aviation business to do our job and look after them, not to abandon them in pursuit of self-interest."* So I got my spoke in. Sixty seconds on the six o'clock national news bulletin. It was important to me because I was incensed at how such appalling hardship could be wilfully visited upon the very people who pay the wages of those occasioning this damage.

Later that Sunday evening, the strike was called off and things looked like getting back to normal by morning. *The Irish Times* Monday editorial was scathing in its criticism of what had been allowed to happen at the airport over the weekend and credited me with the utterance that made the most sense out of a very saturated airwave of soundbites. But it didn't end quite there. I was parking my car at the terminal building with the Pat Kenny radio programme on the radio when I had a "groundhog day" sensation. Here was a senior official of SIPTU trotting out the same old crap I had been listening to now for days. I was fuming and phoned RTÉ. I got through to the producer of the show and minutes later I was in the interview, live from my desk telephone. I went for it. I couldn't bear the thought of what I believed to be outmoded dogma being pumped out to the nation yet again as justification for the unforgivable. Pat Kenny was fair and gave me the platform. By my reckoning, I buried the SIPTU position. I was happy for an instant, but only an instant. Victories were destined to be very short-lived in any given day in the life of Cityjet, before you could count on the next challenge, which was usually only minutes away, engulfing you totally.

Just before I immersed myself in the pressing issues of the day, I took a call from Michael O'Leary. As ever, Michael was not short on coming to the point and, without recounting exactly the colourful way he put it, he was delighted we were on the same side of "this SIPTU nonsense" and "we should work together and go after the rest of all this crap". In pretty clear terms, I told him I wasn't impressed with his very public performances, which had in many ways goaded the union into the action they took. Of course their stance was untenable but while we might share the same view of the unacceptable nature of the near-anarchy that had been brought about by a handful of extreme activists, we were definitely "not on the same side".

The internal daily review meetings we had on the progress of the delivery of the Saab aircraft seemed to throw up more problems than solutions. The list of unresolved issues was growing. It was clear we were dealing with a manufacturer who was not on top of the business of co-ordinating technical support for the aircraft it had produced. When you place an order to lease an aircraft, you are not just dealing with the leasing company. You are in effect buying into a whole system and a complex web of relationships with various commercial entities. In our case, the lessor of the aircraft was a subsidiary of the manufacturer itself but they behaved as if they were not remotely connected. Also, separate contractual arrangements had to be entered into with Allison, the engine manufacturers. There were, as previously mentioned, problems with this engine type. For a start, not enough of them were produced especially in the light of the serviceability shortcomings that were emerging. There was a mandatory extension to the length of prop shaft pending but not enough modification kits yet available from the factory. This would mean regular inspection after every 100 hours of operation until the re-fit had been completed.

The matter of installing the steep approach modification to qualify the aircraft for operations at London City was a problem because Collins, the manufacturer of the avionics suite, were out of stock of the requisite parts. Again it was left to us, the customer of Saab, to sort this out directly. Anybody could be forgiven for thinking that Saab, as the company who designed and put together this airplane and whose badge it wore, would have delivered to their customers on a one-stop-shop basis. The reality was that relationships appeared pretty sour, in some cases, between Saab and the vendors who supplied the various bits that made up the assembled aircraft. In fact, the relationship between Saab Aircraft, the manufacturer, and Saab Leasing also seemed to be fractious most of the time; we witnessed open hostility between these two Saab companies at meetings at which we were present.

Looking back, I suppose what we were seeing was a heretofore highly successful aircraft manufacturer suffering the most acute pain from sudden change of the most unexpected kind. This was a manufacturing giant who invested heavily on the prospect of the Saab 2000 filling the void in the fifty-seat regional market that was not being filled by a jet solution, only to be stuffed by a previously moderately successful manufacturer called Embraer of Brazil. No doubt the Swedes could just about accept defeat by Brazil in soccer, but for one of Sweden's industrial success stories like Saab to be beaten by an emerging minnow from Brazil was a different story. I can now see why Saab were struggling to deliver on our basic pragmatic demands. By this stage, we had gone beyond the "we're your customer and we'll stomp our feet until we get what we want" routine. All we could do was coax and help them to invent solutions. There was no point in expressing shock at the latest service shortcoming or getting mad at people who you know deep down can't do what you need them to do. It was time to be cool but determined to make it happen when it needed to happen.

On the plus side, we had got our act together in a remarkably tight timescale to operate two different aircraft types simultaneously. When the first Saab 2000 arrived in mid-March, we were ready for it and we lost no time in getting it into service on Dublin/London City. We were mixing it in with our BAe 146 service on the route and we were now offering eight return flights per business day. Mixing jets and turboprops on the same route may have worked for Crossair, but was it going to work for us? By the end of March, we were also up and running on the Strasbourg/London City route with the second Saab, transferred from Regional. Our third Saab was delayed and would not be with us until late May, due to the shortage of engines fresh out of overhaul.

One month later, another crisis loomed. We had been operating our first Saab on Dublin/London City with one low-time engine and the second with 3,395 hours on the clock. However, the higher-time engine was subject to a mandatory bulletin from Rolls Royce which called for a compressor movement check every 300 flight hours, which represented about six weeks' activity. Having just completed the check the previous weekend, we received a directive from Rolls Royce telling us to remove the engine from service after fifty more hours, which effectively meant grounding the aircraft by Friday. On top of that, on the same day Saab told us that all the required modifications, like steep approach and anti-skid for London City, had been fitted to our third aircraft, due for delivery at the end of May. However, there were no engines on the aircraft and the two that were due to be swapped from another Saab 2000 being returned by Regional from lease could not now be guaranteed to us, as someone else in Saab Leasing had committed this aircraft, with engines, to Business Air in Scotland. The final piece of good news that day came when Rolls Royce confirmed there was no spare engine available to us to replace the engine we were being forced to remove after only a few weeks of service.

I didn't go ballistic. I just channeled my controlled fury into making very clear demands of Saab at the highest level I could get to. We suffered aircraft downtime for a few days but we got our replacement engine. We also got a guarantee that the two good engines on the returned Regional Airlines aircraft would be fitted to our third Saab. If only that had been the end of our troubles with the Saab 2000. Unlike their Danish neighbours' penchant for producing probably the best beer in the world, these guys could not claim to have made the best aircraft in the world; nor could they claim to offer an acceptable level of support to their unsuspecting airline customers.

When we introduced the Saab, the immediate reaction from our regular passengers on Dublin/London City was pretty blunt. They couldn't understand why we were asking them to "step back in time" and travel on propeller-driven aircraft. They had been used to a jet service and no matter how high-tech and how fast we told them the Saab 2000 was, they just pointed to "those big paddles stuck on to the front of the engines". Another marketing challenge or something much more serious and potentially terminal? The pattern was emerging quickly. Every second flight on the route was with a 146, a very full 146. Meanwhile the Saab flights were dramatically under-performing in bookings.

Our primary objective was to offer a high frequency of flights to our passengers, which meant committing more aircraft to the route. As the 146 was in short supply we had gone for the next best option of supplementing the service with the Saab 2000. The real issue was that we had created a scenario where some of our passengers could choose to ignore the additional frequency of flights and trade preferred time of flight for preferred type of aircraft. Giving your customers a choice that can result in adverse selection against the overall service proposition you are offering is a disaster. The book is wrong on choice being the essence of good marketing.

We worked very hard to correct the public perception of our introducing the Saab 2000 on our blue-riband route. I personally went to visit the senior executives of the most important regular corporate users of our service. Unfortunately, we had also just come through one of our worst periods of technical reliability issues with the 146 since we commenced operations. There was no particular pattern; it was just a really bad run of luck. This in turn created dreadful pressure on our hard-pressed engineering department, who were now supporting two fleets of completely different aircraft types. We had a growing presence at Paris, a contracted-out maintenance service at Strasbourg from Regional and a Stockholm night stop being handled by Malmo Aviation. We could outsource much of this away from base work but as the holder of the operator's certificate, we could never outsource the responsibility.

Anyway, it was hard to create the right kind of listening in the corporate market to the virtues of this sophisticated and ultra-comfortable high-speed turboprop without first of all winning back their confidence in our ability to run an on-time flight schedule on the crucially important business route of Dublin/London City. Thankfully, our Dublin/Paris, Paris/London City, Stockholm/London City and Strasbourg/London City routes were all operating quite well. But Dublin/London City was our flagship service. It was high visibility with the same passengers travelling very often. This was a fence we could not afford to have a hole in for long. There was no magic formula. It took a lot of shoe leather and a high degree of humility combined with an inexhaustible capacity to soak up the brickbats that were hurled our way by disenfranchised customers. But this was our job and this was a hurdle we just had to get over if we wanted to stay in business.

We went back to planning a complete overhaul of the product. We declared war on lateness by introducing a programme which we called "Push on Time". This called for everybody's involvement, from the flight dispatcher to the ground engineers, cockpit crew, cabin crew and baggage handlers. The goal was hitting the scheduled departure time on the nose every time. Where delays were inevitable due to technical failures, we implemented a set of procedures for dealing with passengers in such a way as to improve the quality of the decision-making of frontline staff when it came to a "plan B" scenario.

The heavy maintenance programme on the 146s, coupled with the never-ending fresh costs popping up in connection with getting the Saabs into service, had hammered our cash flow. Added to this was the continued hiring-in of the Flightline 146 to cover for the extended overrun on the work to our own aircraft. We were desperately short of working capital but it was very clear that our shareholders would not be prepared to invest more without a suitable airline equity partner to fill the void left by the departed Malmo Aviation. On the days when I was not immersed in the Saab project and trying to woo back our passengers, I was doing the rounds of secondary banks and aviation financiers in London who entertained the more risky type of covenant, which we very definitely now represented.

Malcolm Holt, an established aircraft broker, was most helpful with introductions to potential partners, among whom was an extraordinary Dutchman called Harry Van Achteren. Harry, through his own investment vehicle, Voyager, took leveraged positions in asset-backed deals. We met often over a short period of weeks. The shape of the evolving deal was complex but on paper looked like a very attractive proposition. It involved the acquisition of Janesville, the specialist leasing company we had set up the previous year in our strategy for generating cash for the airline out of a clever re-financing of two of the aircraft. The investment capital required to fuel the deal would be raised by Voyager and made up of bank debt and a substantial injection of their own cash. Once in control of the leases on the aircraft, Voyager would then release to Cityjet about US$2 million tied up in deposits. This figure would be supplemented by another US$2 million of fresh capital from Voyager. Aidan Keane and myself put an amount of effort into converting the concept into a workable plan. Paul Coulson represented the interests of the Janesville shareholders, who of course were also stakeholders in Cityjet. We got as far as the lawyers drafting agreements, but it never happened. The relationship we had with Harry Van Achteren, which had been showing promising signs of building, somewhere and somehow had begun to dissipate. Harry vanished and so too did any prospect of a much-needed cash injection into Cityjet.

We didn't have time to lament the passing of yet another opportunity to lift the acute financial pressure which by now we had long accepted to be our lot. I knew we had to keep focused on growing the business. We had a momentum going and it was imperative we keep it going. We continued with our planning. By late June, we had finalised details with Air France for the introduction of two 146s on Paris/Florence from the following October. Like London City Airport, Florence was a "146 only" airfield. We would also need to supplement the 146 on Paris/London City with at least thirty per cent of another 146, due to the planned expansion of the flight schedule. Dublin/Paris would continue to account for a minimum of one 146. It was clear that our growing commercial relationship with Air France would depend on our having five identically configured BAe 146 200 series aircraft for the following year. To meet the product specification of Air France would also mean purchasing new six-abreast leather seating, with a folding-down capability of the middle seats to form a coffee table in business class. While we negotiated a higher contract rate with Air France to reflect this additional cost burden, I knew that, at US$300,000 per set of seats as an up-front charge, we would be facing into another large cash crunch not too far down the track.

Chapter Seventeen

OKAY FOR RABBITS, SEND MORE HATS

Our problems with winning back passenger confidence in terms of the on-time performance of our flight schedule continued to be compounded by the appalling reliability of the Saabs. Of course aircraft go unserviceable and we expected a lot of teething problems with an aircraft type we were new to operating. But the real issue here was the dreadful shortcoming in support from the factory in delivering vital spare parts when they were needed. It wasn't so much the number of technical snags as the amount of time to recover from a breakdown that was breaking our hearts and wrecking our business. It was no wonder that, when an unexpected opportunity to acquire a BAe 146 series 100 aircraft on a three-year lease suddenly just popped up, we became instantly engaged. Mechanically identical to our other 146s save for the fact that a shorter fuselage resulted in about three rows fewer seats, it was an old aircraft, being the third one to roll off the production line in the mid-1980s. But no matter, it was a 146 and it had six-abreast seating, giving us the capacity for seventy-seven passengers in a slightly more cramped configuration. This compared to eighty-one passengers on our five-abreast set-up on our four 146 200s. We didn't hang about in declaring our interest in this aircraft. It would alleviate pressure in our very tight flight schedule. The interesting thing about this 146, however, was that its owner was none other than Warren Seymour, the CEO of National Jet

Systems (NJS) of Australia. Warren had of course considered investing in Cityjet some three years earlier.

We threw ourselves into negotiation with Warren and his team and worked out a deal after a lot of hand-to-hand combat. This was how I imagined the velvet-gloved punches must feel when the Aussie rules and Gaelic football teams greet each other in their regular "Compromise Rules" encounter. By this stage we were expert in this business of negotiating the technical details for aircraft leases and executing the agreements in a very short time. There was a lot of work to be done in ensuring that the records were up to spec and that the condition of maintenance would satisfy the Irish Aviation Authority to qualify for inclusion on the Irish register and on our AOC (licence). The aircraft needed a considerable re-fit of equipment to make it compliant with the latest requirements for operations in Europe. We cut a reasonable deal in determining who would pay for what and we just got on with working to get the aircraft delivered in shape to Dublin. Unfortunately, we hit snag after snag with compliance issues, gaps in records and a never-ending list of extended technical modifications. The delivery date was pushed out and out and we began to sense how General Custer and his gallant 7th must have felt as they constantly looked to see if the cavalry was coming over the hill.

Meanwhile we remained under siege on our daily operations. The ongoing tech delays to Saab flights in particular was wreaking havoc. Morale of crew, engineers and all frontline staff was on the floor as they were bearing the brunt of passenger anger. I was busy trying to solve our difficulties at source but I knew I had to stay in very close touch with the mood of our people and to let them know that the job they were doing was invaluable. The management team made themselves accessible to staff and passengers especially in times of flight schedule disruption. I insisted we didn't hide from the problems and we stood firm and responded to each and every passenger complaint. And there were many complaints.

Very much against the recent less-than-encouraging trend, the last Sunday morning in July saw us looking forward to completing our best week of the year for technical performance and passenger loads — and then we got hit not by one aircraft going tech but by *three*, all on the same day. They were fixable problems but enormous delays built up in our schedule. Our biggest issue by evening time was how to perform our last two flights from Dublin to London City and back and not fall foul of the 9.00 pm curfew at City. We launched two 146s within five minutes of each other and we communicated with ATC at London City to get an extension to "closing time" on the understanding that we would perform ten-minute turnarounds. Our first flight landed, off-loaded passengers, re-loaded with a full complement and was airborne for Dublin again within twelve minutes. Our second 146 flight landed at City just five minutes after the earlier one had touched down and repeated this impressive feat of swapping two full loads of passengers against the clock. It took just ten minutes. Clearance to start engines was given and the taxi to the holding point was completed when the command from the tower, incredibly, was to return to the stand and shut down as time was up. We were talking about sixty seconds beyond the extended deadline. Sixty seconds and the aircraft would have been airborne. Sixty seconds which the controller should have been well able to calculate when he gave permission to start-up and taxi to the take-off position. Now we had to tell people they were not going home tonight. We had to de-plane them. Give them back their baggage and then hire and wait for two coaches to come to bring our passengers to a hotel for the night. Our crew would be out of duty hours come the time for the morning departure and the aircraft that was needed to operate out of Dublin for our very heavily booked first flight tomorrow was in the wrong city. Sixty seconds and the pedantic performance of an air traffic controller, who chose not to act pragmatically in caring for passengers who ultimately pay his wages, cost us an incalculable amount of damage and visited a hardship on many people needlessly. I am appalled by management who afford this form of insulation to staff from the effects of any bad decisions they take in the moment.

It was against such a background that I could be forgiven for my subsequent view of London City Airport's contribution in our time of angst. An invitation came some two weeks later to a meeting with their chairman, Ray McSharry, the former EU Commissioner. Mr McSharry laid it on the line that "the Board of directors of the airport are adamant that jets are required" as he applied pressure on me to remove the Saab 2000s. I was quite sure that Moritz Suter, boss of Crossair, did not have to listen to this crap about his Saabs at London City. The memory of that very recent Sunday evening, when we sent in two jets only to have one of them taken prisoner for the night, was still too raw. But I didn't expect that the airport chairman, so far removed from the operational life of the business, would have even the slightest insight into how his airport management and staff could affect a day in the life of one of his busiest customers. "Jets are the thing. Just give us jets."

By the end of August, our fifth 146 finally made it to Dublin and was pressed into service immediately The relief among the exhausted troops was palpable. This was a genuine spare aircraft which was going to be used to plug the gaps caused by other aircraft going tech. And it was being dedicated to getting reliability on Dublin/London City back up to where it needed to be. We now had five 146s and three Saab 2000s. Our reliability and timekeeping began to creep back up. Just like the lag on a jet engine between pushing forward on the throttle, through the spooling up of the blades, until the power surge eventually arrives, so too did our passenger numbers start climbing again. And the prejudice against the Saab began to wane. We had a recovering revenue line but very depleted cash in our tank.

Our strong sense, that September, was that the future of the Dublin/London City route demanded a high frequency and utterly reliable flight schedule. We reckoned that the way to achieve this was to commit three Saab 2000s the following year to an executive shuttle service, offering nine return flights per business day. Also, by making it an all Saab 2000 service, the issues of passenger selection in favour of the jet would be eliminated. All of this was predicated on our being satisfied with the veracity of guarantees of specified technical support which we intended to zealously extract from Saab. We looked forward to the likely progression of the Dublin/East Midlands route and concluded that it could absorb the capacity of the BAe 146 100 series on lease from Warren Seymour and so release a Saab 2000 for Dublin/London City. We still expected to operate a Saab 2000 on Strasbourg/ London City, so that left us looking to acquire at least one more Saab. So, if the plan was to be realised, we would need to end up in 1999 with a fleet of five 146 200 series, one 146 100 series and four or five Saab 2000s — provided we could win the race of revenue capture ahead of the cash draining out. Saab began to burn the late night oil and there was a genuine effort now being made to convince us they could support us adequately were we to operate a fleet of five Saab 2000s by spring of the following year.

The quest for cash took on a renewed urgency. I had continued with my trawl of the secondary banks and aircraft financiers in London to try to replicate the deal we had constructed around some of our aircraft with Janesville the previous year. I was attempting to get a re-financing deal on another of our aircraft, without the support of shareholders subscribing to the arrangement. Essentially I was looking for close to one hundred per cent finance. It couldn't be done. So it was back to the well once more. I started on a campaign of convincing Janesville, whose shareholders were common to the airline, to repeat the exercise they had engaged in previously. I worked on Anglo Irish Bank again and finally, by late September, we had a deal that saw Janesville purchase the last of our US Air leased 146s and lease it back into Cityjet. Again there was a cash release to the airline, made possible by re-financing to the market value, which was comfortably ahead of the sale price from US Air.

In the weeks leading up to pulling off this latest "rabbit out of hat" interim financial remedy, we had a bizarre sideshow running with Franco Mancusola, the founder and CEO of Debonair. He had raised an enormous amount of money, reputed to be about stg£30 million, to launch his airline, which boasted a fleet of about ten 146s, all on lease from US Air. Franco's base was Luton and he operated scheduled services to various cities in Spain and Germany. Uniquely, his schedule resembled a race-track type pattern; not only did he offer point-to-point flights between Luton and these destinations, he also connected some of these destination points with each other. Franco had been successful in raising seed capital, particularly in Germany, and very quickly went for a listing on the AIMS market. The amount of cash Debonair had at their disposal was the talk and the envy of the regional airline sector. But like most things in this business, so too were the huge losses he was racking up, as the Debonair depressed load factors were pretty common knowledge also. Lacking a strategic partner, Debonair had no established distribution network. Debonair at that time were depending on internet bookings which had not quite caught on as the dynamic channel it is today for airline reservations. They had no code share arrangements with other more established airlines which would have made selling seats a lot easier. Also, they were thinly spread across different countries due to their ambitiously expansive route network and they didn't have the people on the ground building relationships with travel agents to promote their flights ahead of the incumbent players. Added to this was the fact that Franco was promoting a low-fares model with, as we knew only too well, a relatively high operating cost aircraft type in the form of the 146.

Franco appeared unannounced into my office one late summer afternoon. We talked and agreed to have a number of meetings between our respective senior people over the coming weeks to see if we could find a piece of common ground for combining our operations with a view to producing a winning formula. If I had €50,000 for every *déjà vu* moment I have had with yet another "potential new partner", I probably wouldn't be writing this book but an entirely different one on how to get rich through advising people to stay out of the airline business. But back to Franco. There he was, larger than life, speaking the speak. I convinced myself once more, *you never know what might just happen next in these scenarios*. With eyes very wide open and intent on keeping count of the number of fingers I had on each hand after the flesh-pressing formalities, I entered into this zany dialogue with Franco and his lieutenant.

When somebody says to me, in the early phase of a negotiation, that they "have no sacred cows", I know they mean the exact opposite. Franco was assuring me he wasn't going to have any particular hang-ups on whose licence we used, theirs or ours, whose airline name, whose head office, whose operational base, etc. But, of course, he had a whole herd of sacred cows and he would not be able to conceal his control freak tendencies for very much beyond our second or third subsequent meeting. I rest my case on Franco's "open state of mind" with his suggested fair and equitable solution for naming the proposed merged operation. His wife, who he claimed was of Irish extraction, had come up with the brilliant idea of spelling the "air" in Debonair with a Gaelic "e". Debonaer was Franco's idea of parity of identity in our "joint venture" operation.

We didn't fail to make progress on potentially banging the two airlines together over something as trite as the name of the new airline. Franco wanted to pick up on the good things we had, like the relationship with Air France, which afforded us a balance between our "own risk" scheduled routes, Air France-franchised routes and contract flying for Air France. He also recognised that we had a relatively cost-effective operating base and highly professional flight operations and engineering departments. But —

and it was a big but — Franco could not see the necessity of dramatically reducing his loss-making route network and moving the combined operation to the balanced-type model we had gone well down the road on already. We were still losing money but our rate of losses were tumbling down. Debonair was burning cash at a frightening rate but we felt he still had enough to propel a merged entity forward and into early profitability. We never got to find out if he had the bottle for it. Talks broke down and, to be honest, we had so many other issues we simply could not afford to hang around to determine if any trace of life could be found in the corpse of the collapsed dialogue. As ever, we moved on. Debonair did indeed die the following year when that staggering amount of cash eventually ran out. Ironically, in their dying months they had substituted operating a number of their loss-making routes for contract flying for Swissair, but perhaps by then it was too late.

Chapter Eighteen

DESPERATE FOR FUEL

Notwithstanding our latest aircraft finance deal, which put us in much-needed funds, we were desperately seeking serious investment to get us to the point of gearing up for the expanded Air France programme for the next year. We had our list of usual suspects from the airline community, such as Air France themselves, or Brit Air to whom Air France had recently introduced us with a broad hint of a possibility of an equity link-up. We also were developing good contacts with Jersey European who operated for Air France in addition to their own route network. And then there was National Jet and Warren Seymour who had re-entered our lives through the lease of his 146 100 series. Schreiner Airways are a Dutch company with extensive interests in aviation, ranging from franchised airline operations, helicopter services to the oil industry and pilot training. We talked intensely over a two-week period. Again, here was another potentially promising situation. They were very professional people with a great business. We were interesting to them but the pace at which we needed a deal to happen was always going to be a lot quicker than they needed to go with. Our focus would have to shift to someone we thought we could get a deal with sooner if we were to stave off a bad ending. Outside of an airline partner, there were a few remote possibilities, including an interesting businessman from Nuremberg called Hans Rudolf Worhl who had the rare distinction of actually liking the Saab 2000. He had a huge interest in our relationship with Air France but he made it a precondition of his investment that we get the French to take a 25 per cent stake in Cityjet. I could not guarantee this, even though I felt we were getting close to that point where a sufficient level of dependency by Air France on Cityjet could be established. As ever in business, it was about timing and this was ahead of what I could deliver just then. He was a player, though, as he subsequently demonstrated in 2002 when he took over DBA, formerly Deutsche BA.

By the end of October 1998, Warren Seymour and Adele Lloyd were back in Dublin. Warren was working on an aggressive plan to start up a BAe 146 operation in Italy under a British Airways franchise. He was confident of attracting Italian investment to augment what Adele and himself were going to provide. One of the big obstacles the Australians wanted to overcome was the complexity and attendant expense associated with obtaining an Italian aircraft operators' certificate (AOC). Their clear preference was for an Irish AOC and Cityjet, of course, already had one of those. They had begun the process of preliminary application to the Irish Aviation Authority (IAA) for their own Irish AOC, which would be under the name of National Jet Ireland (NJI) but they also initiated talks with us about a potential investment in Cityjet with the intention of expanding to cover the proposed Italian operation. This was going to be difficult, especially as the mainstay of Cityjet's business was a growing relationship with Air France. For Cityjet to fly simultaneously in the colours of British Airways and Air France would be stretching the limits of where these arch-rivals would be prepared to go. I was instinctively worried about the effect this British Airways connection would have on the French as I remained absolutely certain that Air France held the key to Cityjet's survival in the longer term.

We came up with a potential scheme which would see the conversion of Cityjet, the AOC holder, to a central air transport operating company which we would refer to as Cityjet AOC. With this entity at the centre, there would then be a holding company called Italiana Holdings which would hold the franchise with BA for the proposed new operation in Italy. There would also be City-jet Holdings which would hold the contracts and franchise agreements with Air France. Both Cityjet Holdings and Italiana Holdings would wet-lease aircraft from Cityjet AOC and run their respective routes under the appropriate colours. The distinct advantage of this type of set-up was huge cost savings. With a centralised licence came a centralised maintenance department, flight operations centre and common training. Effectively, we would be running two airlines with only one set of fixed administration costs. As the common aircraft type to both operations would be the BAe 146, there would also be enormous incremental benefits brought about by scale. To avoid conflict between Air France and BA, the plan was for the Cityjet AOC company to have separate standalone management, whose sole interaction with Cityjet Holdings and Italiana Holdings would be to supply them each with aircraft and crew together with all technical support needed to keep the planes flying. There was a complication. Warren and Adele were adamant they wanted majority control of Cityjet AOC. As non-Europeans they could not hold more than 49.9 per cent of an EU-licensed airline.

As always with Cityjet, we could never count on one big deal coming off which would be the answer to our problems. We had to continue to grind out the day-to-day operation of the airline and pursue every possible avenue of salvation if we were to stay alive long enough to find the right partner. The Saab saga rumbled on. Would we, could we afford to stay with this aircraft type? Staying with it meant in effect moving up to a fleet of five Saab 2000s in addition to five 146s. Getting out meant settling a sizable debt which we had run up with Saab on technical support and spare parts. Termination would also trigger the forfeiture of our security deposits on the leases. We got positive and entered into negotiations. There was only one direction to go in as there was no percentage in deploying reverse thrust at this stage. But taking more aircraft would mean exposing our financial position and Saab had been asking difficult questions of late as we continued to stall on talking about our debt repayment. We assured them we would have a new shareholder on board by year end.

Meanwhile the Cityjet board of directors were becoming cautiously optimistic about the prospect of Warren Seymour and Adele Lloyd making a substantial investment in the airline. The fact that the Australians already owned National Jet Systems, which operated a fleet of more than twenty 146s on a Qantas franchise on domestic routes down under, meant there would be a wealth of experience coming on top of the investment. The mood was to push for confirmation of their intent. Warren produced Speedwing, the BA consultancy arm, as his agents to conduct due diligence on Cityjet ahead of his committing funds. My biased impression of Speedwing, admittedly formed at a distance up to now, was that it was the "Dad's Army" section through which rutted senior middle management in BA were unleashed on unsuspecting airlines who were in desperate need of expertise on a consultancy basis.

Speedwing went about their investigative work and Warren did his hopping between Dublin, London to see BA and Rome to get his Italian investors lined up for his Italiana adventure. But he was also required back in Oz because he was still the CEO of NJS. I was uncomfortable. Speedwing had finished their interim investigation and I presumed they had furnished a report to the Australians. I couldn't get a straight "yes" or "no" out of Warren as to whether he was coming in or not.

I got him on the phone in Adelaide. It was a frustrating conversation, not made easier by his abrasive style. He had the Speedwing report but he hadn't read it yet. He would discuss things with Adele and call Paul Coulson, our chairman, within twenty-four hours. I told him I was under intense pressure with Saab as I was in the middle of critical negotiations, which were on a knife edge. They could pull the plug and sink us and yet all anybody had to say, including off-the-cuff comments by Speedwing, was that "the Saabs have to go". That was fine in theory but they happened to make up almost one-third of our fleet and we had security deposits at risk and a debt to Saab to take care of. I pushed hard in the conversation for an answer. "Have you gone cold on us?" I asked. "I need to know now if its no." He assured me he hadn't gone cold.

Three days later, I was jostling my way through the crowd behind the back of the West Stand at Lansdowne Road with Jane when my jacket pocket rang. It was Warren and he wasn't looking for odds on the All Blacks' score against Ireland, which was due to start in a few minutes. It was noisy but I could just about make out that he was upbeat and feeling positive about going forward with us. He wanted control of Cityjet. He would take on the 146s on lease from Janesville and give a five-year commitment on the leases. He would help us resolve the Saab issue and he didn't want to take on any responsibility for historic debts. Not exactly what I wanted to hear but he was engaging. My mood improved and held good — even after we lost a match we could have won, if rugby was played for only seventy minutes and not eighty.

The next day I went to Paris to acquaint Air France with the intricate issues surrounding our continuing operation of the Saabs. Earlier that morning, I met with Proteus Airlines, a French regional who Air France were moving very close to. Proteus needed two Saab 2000 aircraft to satisfy Air France on specific contract routes they were operating. They were exploring how we might re-deploy aircraft and crews to operate for them. Air France were helpful. They had confidence that winter 1999 would see large demand for fifty-seat high-speed turboprops in the domestic network due to the impending defection of an Air France regional partner airline. They felt that the Proteus short-term need could help us bridge this time span and give us the reassurance we needed to commit to staying with the type. It was encouraging.

A week in most businesses is a week, not such a big deal. In an airline, it can be a generation. In Cityjet's life, a week could bring unbelievable change. And so it was: one week later, Warren dropped his bomb. He wasn't going to invest in Cityjet. The wise men of Speedwing had produced their final version of the report. The Saabs had to go and, as if we didn't know it already, there "was an urgent requirement of funds". What he would do was provide Cityjet with between four and six BAe 146s which we would place on our AOC, and operate on a wet-lease basis for his Italian franchise with BA for a fee to be agreed. As had happened so many times in the past, we were too busy with the business of being in business to be disappointed. We were also focused on how to step up to the plate in terms of the dramatic expansion opportunity Air France were putting in front of us from the start of the new season, which was then only three months away, pro-vided of course we would still be around then. But I still had enough emotional disk space to feel anger at being dicked around. This wasn't a deal. It was useless. Our answer was "no". We knew one thing. Warren had got himself so far down the runway with his Italian franchise concept, with a target start date of March, also only three months away, that he didn't have a whole lot of op-tions of getting his show in the air. He had no immediate prospect of a European AOC. He had the promise of Italian investors to put in much-needed cash and he would need to demonstrate progress to keep their interest. He was almost there with BA on the grant-ing of the franchise and he was burning cash keeping all of these plates spinning at the same time.

We sweated but we were sure he was too. That same week, Air France came back to us to declare that in their opinion the Saab 2000 was a good aircraft and they felt they could make good use of a small fleet of them operated by Cityjet on possible routes to Germany to replace other operators with Dornier 328s and ATR 42s. You couldn't bank it but it was helpful, especially as Aidan Keane and myself were preparing for a crucial make-or-break date with Saab in Stockholm in seven days' time.

There was some contact between Paul Coulson and Warren during the following week, which began to build towards a "maybe". Coincidentally, 17 December, the same day Aidan and myself ploughed our way through a snowstorm in a taxi from the airport into downtown Stockholm, we had been told to expect an answer form Oz ahead of our meting with Saab. No call came and I decided to switch my mobile off once we entered the Saab building. I figured at that point that we didn't need to be burdened with bad news.

I was reminded of a true story that had happened a few years earlier. Accompanied by my daughters Sarah and Eleanor, I had flown my Cessna Skylane, "Charlie Alpha Papa", to Shannon on a summer's afternoon. I parked alongside a single-engined Cessna Centurion, which I noticed had a large ferry fuel tank taking up most of the cabin. The really curious thing was that all of the engine instruments were covered by adhesive paper. Shortly afterwards, I was in air traffic control to file my return flight plan to Dublin when I asked the guy I was dealing with about the aircraft with the blanked instruments. "Oh, that's just come in from the US on a ferry flight to Switzerland. In fact, the pilot is over there." With that, our man turned to join in the conversation. "Well," I asked him, "what's the story with the blanked out gauges?" He fixed me with a stare and then the long drawl of his mid-western accent followed. "It's like this. When I get out over the ocean and reach a point with just about as much water behind me as ahead of me, the way I figure it is I just don't want any bad news when there is nothing much I can do about it anyway!"

Back in Stockholm: of the very many tough meetings I was involved in over the years, this one sticks in my memory as one of the hardest to navigate through. Going in, we knew we were in dire straits and unless there was an immediate injection of cash into the company, we were going under within a matter of weeks. And this did not include the debt of some $700,000 due to Saab. Against this was our deeply felt sense of indignation at the dreadfully poor level of technical support from Saab, as the manufacturer of the aircraft. Over the eight months of operation of the aircraft type, which accounted for thirty-five per cent of the total Cityjet fleet, more than fifty per cent of all technical disruptions were recorded by Saabs. We also were acutely aware that if Warren Seymour did end up in control of Cityjet, the prospects of Saabs being retained were likely to be short-lived. On the other hand, we had to promote our absolute certainty of an impending investor if we were to scratch out any kind of a decent deal with Saab and stay their hand from any precipitous action on fore-closing on our debt and compromising the leases on the existing aircraft.

To compound the cocktail swirling around in our heads, we were mindful that Air France actually saw a future for even more Saabs and so we also had to engage in worthwhile dialogue to open up the prospect of more aircraft being made available during the following year. More Saabs could only happen if Cityjet was to be re-capitalised, and if cash was to come from the Australians it wouldn't necessarily be used to get more Saabs. The French were pivotal in the forward viability of Cityjet and we certainly didn't want to risk that relationship by way of another breakdown with an aggressive new shareholder, as the memory of the Swedish assault some eighteen months earlier was still too fresh in the minds of those who matter in Paris.

So, as we sat down we were very conscious we were embarking on an elephant-eating exercise and we were determined to avoid indigestion by taking very small bites. We had a four-point plan going in which was:

- Agree the debts to both Saab Aircraft and Saab Leasing;

- Negotiate the best possible terms of repayment over time;

- Secure assurances on ongoing technical support of a superior quality than heretofore;

- Agree on the Saab fleet size going forward.

It was time to roll the dice and see how far we would get. We came out of Stockholm with as reasonable a deal as we could hope for in the circumstances of our stretched cash position. We got some forgiveness on quantum; not a lot, but we did get to spread our repayments over the next six months. We also managed to kick out the issue of fleet expansion to a position of not likely to happen before autumn of the following year, consistent with the Air France demand for more fifty-seater lift. On the question of our new investor, we bluffed our way through, conveying that it simply wasn't in doubt but just being held up by last minute due diligence issues and paperwork.

Arriving back in Dublin with just seven days to Christmas Day, we got word from Australia that investment of IR£3.5 million was on. There would be conditions, including our having to play a centre-stage role in fast-tracking the obtaining of an Irish AOC for the proposed "Italian job". The only way to accomplish this was to make the application a mirror copy of what we had in place for Cityjet. We also would be required to submit to an involvement by the Speedwing consultants over a period of weeks as they would go about planning a restructuring of the business of Cityjet. A "Heads of Terms" agreement was executed over the fax between Warren Seymour and our chairman, Paul Coulson, and a promise was made that we would receive the first down-payment of £0.75 million on 22 December, with staged payments of the remaining £2.75 million over the following six weeks.

It was after 11.30 that Christmas Eve morning when I made my third call to Hugh Rodgers, our battle-scarred Financial Controller, who instead of heading north to his family in Donegal, was still in the office awaiting confirmation from the bank that the money had arrived up from down under. Bingo, at last it was there. Elation? No, absolutely not. Why? I couldn't say then, but I probably have a better understanding of my emotional state looking back from here. I was sure of one thing: as yet another odds-defying Christmas in the life of Cityjet as a living, breathing airline was clocked up, this didn't smell good and it certainly didn't feel in the remotest way like the ideal solution. It just didn't feel like the problem had been fixed, especially as it seemed very much like we were just a sideshow to what our new investor was really going for with his proposed BA franchise in Italy. Circumstances once more were compelling me to suspend my good nose for these things in the interests of getting a result. But that nose was to come to the rescue before too many weeks of the new year had been consumed.

Chapter Nineteen

You're not Dropped, But You can't Play on Saturday

Anticipating how to get down to business with your new investors in the life of senior management in any company being acquired would probably be the single biggest preoccupation of the corporate collective consciousness. But in the day-to-day affairs of an incredibly busy regional airline, like Cityjet, there was always a whole lot going on, both internally and externally. Notwithstanding the scheduling of the next board meeting for 11 January, at which we would formally agree to the new investment, we still pressed on with the sourcing of additional BAe 146 aircraft to step up to the expanded programme with Air France, which was now only eleven weeks away. We were also negotiating a substantial loan from the French to cover the cost of installing the flexible six-abreast seating, with the middle seat folding down in business class into a coffee table. At US$300,000 per aircraft, persuading the French to advance us this money was the only way we could achieve the refurbishment in line with their cabin product standard.

We had heard of an identical 146 series 200 to ours being potentially available for sale from a most unlikely source, Titan Airways. Titan were an operator out of Stansted who had two 146s and two or three ATR 42s . They were in the business of providing aircraft and crew to substitute for airlines with an aircraft unexpectedly out of service. We were a very regular customer of Titan, as we unfortunately had to avail of their services far too many times over the previous six years. Owned and managed by Gene Wilson, Titan were as mean as they come. Completely inflexible, Wilson seemed to take the simple view that his customers were really screwed when they made a call to Titan in the first place, so he just turned the screw as tight as he wanted on price and conditions. We didn't exactly expect a bargain when it came to him putting one of his 146s up for sale. The price, at US$7.0 million, was the price and anyone who cared could take it or leave it. And the state of maintenance was also as the buyer would find it, which in this case was only a few weeks away from its scheduled "C" check. A "C" check is a mandatory inspection of an aircraft which must take place every year and depending on what's discovered can take from a minimum of ten days to an average of two weeks to complete. It is a thorough examination of the entire mechanics and general condition of the airframe.

In the industry it is normal to offer an aircraft for sale fresh out of a "C" check but nothing about Wilson's style could be described as being normal. So a buyer would have to accept the price as it stood and take a flyer on how much the "C" check would cost in terms of component replacement. This could run from US$150,000 to US$400,000, depending on how your luck held out. The availability of this aircraft was tempting but the fact that there would be no negotiation on price and that we would have to underwrite the "C" check didn't fill us with a sense of getting a great commercial deal. We mentally filed it under the firm category of "maybe, but not just yet". Besides, shareholder support would be needed to help finance the purchase and we were up to our necks in trying to resolve who exactly our shareholders were going to be as we continued with our "on again, off again" Australian courtship.

As we embraced the first days of yet another year as an operating airline, we pushed ahead with the spade work on the AOC application for Warren's "Italian job". We also got down to detail with Air France on the negotiation of a new franchise deal on Dublin/Paris and the putting in place of logistics to support our growing maintenance station at CDG. The recruitment of more pilots and cabin crew was also a major preoccupation, as we needed to act now in order to have sufficient numbers for the start of the expanded programme with Air France, including the now high-frequency service between Florence and Paris, by the end of March.

Soon enough, 11 January came around and the Board sat in the company of the new shareholders. It wasn't a happy meeting for me. The manner of the inward investment was not straightforward. A newly formed special purposes holding company known as Girner Limited was to grant loans to Cityjet. Girner would receive its funding from Warren Seymour and Adele Lloyd. The Australians aspired to owning sixty per cent of the stock in return for the funding they were bringing. I was adamant in my interpretation of the EU regulations governing ownership of airlines that non-EU nationals could not hold more than forty-nine per cent of the stock in an EU-registered airline. I suggested that they should loan to Girner an additional amount equivalent to the value of eleven per cent of the stock in Cityjet which, if remaining unpaid after two years, would convert to equity, which would be placed in the hands of EU nationals approved by the Irish regulatory authorities. I was not troubled with these mechanics of investment as long as they listened to the importance of staying within the rules.

What really bugged me, though, was the insistence of Warren Seymour that the Speedwing team be brought in to effectively run the airline during the "re-structuring phase". David Cooper of Speedwing would be appointed Acting General Manager and I would remain figuratively in the role of Accountable Manager. I was furious. I objected strenuously and forced a record of my concern to be written into the minutes. I had two issues with the proposal. The investment was not remotely complete, as only £0.75 million out of £3.5 million had been paid in at this point; and I refused to be exposed as the Accountable Manager to the authorities

by any executive decisions being made by David Cooper as Acting
General Manager. But even more than this was the deep sense of
losing the confidence of the board. They knew just how hard I had
battled to keep the company alive, to continue to make us look attractive enough to Air France to be favoured with more flying
programmes and to keep us in the shape of a viable airline worthy
of fresh investment support. Yet here were two potential investors
coming to the table with only twenty per cent of the money they
had promised being produced so far and I was expected to step
aside and let "the experts" from British Airways get on with it.

I then had to listen to some fighting talk from Warren about
sorting Saab out and getting rid of the turboprops, closing down
the Dublin/East Midlands route and reducing staff headcount by
one hundred. It was shatteringly obvious that the new messiah
was being given the keys and I was expected to just go along with
whatever way he wanted to call it. Of course we needed fresh
funds desperately, but the price of support from this particular
source was becoming ominously clear to me. Cityjet would be
used to serve Warren's ambitions in Italy as a British Airways
franchisee. He was imposing a British Airways management team
on us and yet he had only made a down-payment on his investment. I was far from confident that we would see the rest of the
money but the worrying thing was that he would be allowed to
re-shape Cityjet to serve his Italian agenda in the meanwhile. I
was especially nervous around what this was going to do to our
relationship with Air France, which was finally poised to become
a very meaningful partnership for the long term.

There had been many low points in the story of getting Cityjet
into the air and keeping it there against impossible odds, but this
was for me, very painfully, the absolute lowest rung on the ladder
of emotions I had experienced since the whole thing began as an
idea back in 1992. Quite simply, I had completely lost the confidence of the board, who were now entrusting the management of
the airline to a comparative stranger who was distracted hugely

by his efforts to establish an operation in Italy. The puppet regime being put in place was made up of near-retirement-age middle-ranked ex-management people in British Airways, none of whom had ever run a regional airline. This really couldn't be happening, but the sick feeling that had taken up permanent residence in my stomach told me that it was.

In the weeks that followed, my worst fears about the lack of effective management capability of the Speedwing people was confirmed graphically and Warren, as predicted, was increasingly making interventions from the end of his mobile, which was always somewhere between London and Rome as he became buried under the pressures of getting his Italian BA franchise to the starting line. I knew that these guys from Speedwing were so off the pace of what we had found to be the required level of performance to keep things happening. My intuition told me that they would cock up somewhere quite quickly. Meanwhile, I continued to keep Air France happy as we progressed towards the expanded flying programme, due to start now in less than nine weeks. And then the first own goal was scored by David Cooper, who just had to go and announce himself in Paris to Air France as the new Acting General Manager of Cityjet. I had warned him about the sensitivities of any BA connection, but twenty-four hours after his visit I received a fax from Air France of the Speedwing/British Airways business card David Cooper left with them.

I took my cue and penned a very blunt note to Paul Coulson and the other Irish directors. I told them in plain writing that to date only £0.75 million had been received from the Australians. They had missed the £1 million due two weeks previously and a further £1 million was due in two days' time, with the final £0.75 million due two weeks after that. I attached a sheet of creditor commitments we had to meet immediately, which showed an urgent requirement for at least £1 million. I advised that the Department of Public Enterprise, who held responsibility for licensing issues for airlines, were looking for up-to-date financial information on Cityjet and full disclosure on the details of the investment by the Australians.

Apart from my obvious concern over the lack of cash resources, I advised the directors that I was bothered by the fact that we as a Board of Directors had passed executive authority in the management of Cityjet to Warren Seymour and his agents ahead of their living up to the undertaking in relation to cash injection. It was evident to me that Warren Seymour's clear priority was to get National Jet Ireland up and running with an Irish licence and BAe 146 300 series aircraft from Taiwan. I felt he was acting as an absentee landlord on the end of a mobile phone who refused to delegate authority to his agents or subordinates at Cityjet.

By default or design, we were witnessing an ongoing due diligence ahead of cash commitment, which was not a precondition of the agreement. Meanwhile the credibility of Cityjet and my personal credibility were being stretched beyond reasonable bounds in terms of exposure with the regulatory authorities, most particularly as a result of our efforts to procure an AOC for NJI by way of cloning the Cityjet licence. I pointed out that Warren went contrary to my advice by nominating himself as the CEO and Accountable Manager for NJI on the formal AOC application to the IAA. His nomination was duly rejected by the IAA some days later.

I poured out my frustration to the directors. I was aggravated that there was a lack of appreciation that Cityjet was not a start-up airline but had commitments and deadlines to stick to, most notably the expanded Air France programme.

The Business Plan had been in existence for some months and while there was broad agreement on the projected activity, time had been lost in quantifying the resources levels going forward. Here we were, knee-deep in experts, which we accepted as part of the investment process. But what I could not accept was the lack of any apparent plan of action in getting to key decisions and cut-off dates. Instead, we were being subjected to an ongoing meandering analysis of functions to the detriment of making the urgent transformation of the airline to an Air France partner.

Our priority had to be one of securing two aircraft if we were to honour our undertakings with Air France. We also had to dedicate ourselves to the task of transferring our entire distribution system to Air France for all our routes. I concluded my rant by reporting the emergence of an unnecessary threat to our Air France relationship through David Cooper's carelessness in passing his Speedwing business card into the hands of senior Air France management in Paris. I was incensed at this especially as we had warned Brian Carradine, as the Speedwing project leader, of the dangers of flashing Speedwing cards anywhere near the French. I called for a frank discussion on what immediate steps might be taken to secure adequate funding for the company forward in the event that the Australians failed to honour their commitment.

We certainly had a full exchange at the next day's meeting and I undertook to draft a critical path plan immediately, which was duly circulated that evening to directors. While it seemed I was being listened to, there was no move to fire Speedwing and *tell* Warren that all bets were off. I was beginning to despair as to how many smoking guns I had to produce to get unequivocal support from the directors for the actions that needed to be taken, and taken very fast.

There were other sideshows running that would have a significant bearing on the outcome of this scary scenario. The aircraft financier I had referred to in my note to directors was another Australian by the name of Luke Butler. He had been parachuted in on us by Warren Seymour some days earlier accompanied by his girlfriend. On learning, by phone, that Butler was going to arrive, I asked Warren for some background. I was informed that he didn't know him particularly well but he was confident he would be leasing the aircraft from him. Warren asked me to give Butler every assistance in introducing him to the right contacts.

Tall, lean, tanned and long-leather-coated, Butler was, to my eyes and ears, certainly not what he was purporting to be. So strong was my hunch that after only ten minutes I excused myself and took Aidan Keane out of the room with me to compare assessments of this guy. We were convinced that this Luke Butler was spoofing and was in all likelihood a conman. We returned to the meeting and listened as Butler represented to us that he was the purchaser of the five BAe 146s from Uni-Air of Taiwan and he would be leasing them to NJI for the BA Italian franchise operation. He told us that on Warren's advice he was going to use the services of A&L Goodbody and KPMG to help establish an Irish leasing company. He asked us to reserve accommodation at the Shelbourne Hotel on his behalf and for his account and he took his leave with girlfriend in tow. It was not the last I would hear of him.

The next week I received a call from my longstanding contact in Anglo Irish Bank to ask me what I could tell him about a Luke Butler who had approached them for US$60 million financing on five BAe 146s from Taiwan. I told him I could not vouch in any way for him and that I suspected he was not what he represented himself to be. The following words were much-needed music to my tired ears: "Our background search indicates he may have been involved in an aircraft transaction scam in Australia."

I went into overdrive. I contacted our insurance brokers in London, who I had been in very close contact with at that time, to fight off the predatory attempts of Nelson Hurst, a rival London-based broker, to take the business from them. The aviation insurance market is very tightly knit and very well informed on gossip. Within minutes I was given a name to call. Neil Hansford, yet another Australian, but operating for a number of years out of the UK, was an aviation consultant. Neil had been a former director of Ansett Airlines and TNT and it turned out that he personally had been responsible for putting in the liquidator to Butler Aircraft Services Limited, a Butler-controlled enterprise. Hansford told me that Luke Butler's trail of destruction went back as far as

1987 and there was a video copy available of an Australian TV programme on him. It transpired that the internet was full of stories of his adventures. His scams followed a pattern: he would purport to be an experienced aviation financier entering a new jurisdiction to establish a special-purpose leasing company. Local lawyers and accountants would get hired, paper would be produced and deposits taken from unsuspecting third parties to secure aircraft deliveries. Sadly the aircraft would never appear, the deposits would not be returned and Butler would leave town trailing unpaid bills, his pockets full of other people's cash.

I called one of the partners in A&L Goodbody. Too late. There was about £20,000 worth of time charged on the clock for laying down the paperwork for the establishment of the leasing company. KPMG hadn't been taken for as much. And then there was the Shelbourne Hotel. "Has Mr Butler settled his account?" (We knew the assistant manager well.) "No, and there's quite a lot of money on the tab." The hotel management started to push Butler to settle his bill but he quite arrogantly brushed all requests for payment aside. Eventually, Butler's father, whose contact details were furnished by his errant son, coughed up long distance by credit card.

Bizarrely, in the midst of absorbing what I was learning about Butler, he called to my office on the afternoon of 5 February to tell me that Warren Seymour had asked him on the previous Tuesday for a loan of money in order that Warren could fulfil his investment undertaking to Cityjet. I was livid. I composed a note to Paul Coulson in which I laid out everything I had discovered about Butler and I expressed my utter dismay that Warren Seymour knew nothing about this man who apparently had a colourful reputation in aviation circles in Australia. It was obvious that if Warren was relying on this con artist to provide him with aircraft for the Italian operation due to start in April, then there would be no Italian gig. I also expressed my concern that Butler could have been made privy to the full details of the deal, which would have the effect of seriously compromising us with a crook. This was to prove to be all too prophetic within a matter of days.

To complicate matters, Warren had finally responded to the intense pressure Paul Coulson had been applying for him to perform on his commitment to inject cash into Cityjet. On 5 February, £1 million was received into Girner, who in turn would lend it to Cityjet. This was the payment due on 14 January. So now a total of £1.75 million had been received, with an equal amount still outstanding. Warren committed to Paul to pay over the remaining monies by 14 February but he also wanted a meeting in London to discuss things. Paul met him on 11 February armed with the knowledge about Butler and his alleged request from Warren for funding to help close the deal on Cityjet. It was an intense meeting, by all accounts, with Warren accepting that Butler could have no further part to play in any of his dealings and that he would immediately take up the issue of alternative aircraft leases for the Italian operation with British Aerospace Asset Management.

Meanwhile, I was to head up the effort of getting two additional 146s for the expanded Air France programme. The Saab deal negotiated by Aidan Keane and myself back in December was to stand although we would attempt to negotiate some improvements. But the big issue was the remaining £1.75 million. Warren finally admitted he couldn't produce this money but he had another investor in London who was prepared to invest within a week. This was predicated on the investor approving the Speedwing business plan, which still hadn't been produced, and the board of Cityjet approving the credentials of the investor.

Chapter Twenty

IT'S NEVER OVER

I wasn't happy. Yes, Paul Coulson was moving back towards lending me support and believing in my sense of direction again. However, Warren was still being regarded as in a position of power and my management team still had to endure a bunch of wasters in the tent in the form of the Speedwing people. I wrote yet another note to the directors. In it, I chronicled the events of the past few weeks and referred to the Critical Path Plan I had previously prepared, which was being made subordinate to the Speedwing Business Plan, which was still not finalised. In the light of everything that had come to pass, much of which had been alluded to in my previous note to the directors, I requested that the board terminate the agreement with Warren and that Warren and Speedwing be removed from executive office immediately. I sought an urgent and unequivocal endorsement by the board of directors of my authority to discharge my executive duties as the CEO of Cityjet.

Without waiting for a reply, I went to a meeting in Luton, set up for me by Neil Hansford. I was given the opportunity to present to Chris Foyle and his senior team at Air Foyle. Christopher Foyle was well known, both in publishing circles as the heir to the famous Foyle's bookshop in London, and in the flying world as the man who operated those enormous Antonov freighters around the world, moving out-sized cargo loads. In effect, Air Foyle wasn't actually an airline but more of an aircraft operating company. They had a licence which allowed them operate aircraft but they always did so on behalf of others. For example, Easyjet started on the Air Foyle AOC with Air Foyle crew and engineers. I spent four hours in the boardroom selling the opportunity of Air Foyle coming in to complete the investment Warren had not concluded. I was confident there was no chance Warren or any proxy on his behalf would produce the outstanding money. I got them very excited around the Air France relationship and our move towards full airline partner status with the French giant. Neil Hansford was there in his capacity of special adviser to Chris Foyle on aviation opportunities. Neil was sold on the idea and was pressing his client hard.

The opportunity for Air Foyle was timely, as the termination dates on a couple of substantial contracts they had in place with third-party operators were imminent. Although Air Foyle had never been directly in the scheduled airline business in their own right, the idea of taking a majority stake in Cityjet was appealing to them.

They wanted to do a three-day due diligence in Dublin and if everything I told them stacked up, Chris Foyle said he would do it. Doing it now meant coming up with IR£6 million. I got back that afternoon and I told Paul Coulson what I had done and asked for an answer to my note to the directors. Although somewhat shocked at what I had managed to conjure up by way of Air Foyle coming to look us over and understandably a little wary of a potential "here we go again" episode, he gave me the nod. He knew it was pointless giving Warren any more time and he agreed with going all out for what was certainly our last real hope of pulling something out of the fire.

I took pleasure in giving the Speedwing boys their packing orders although I had grown fond of David Cooper, who secretly was very supportive of what we were trying to do. I was now on high-octane fuel as it was a race against the clock to see if we could complete the Air Foyle investment while securing the Titan

146 purchase and negotiate the purchase of the 146 we had on lease from Malmo Aviation since their departure at the end of 1997. And there was still another aircraft to be found. Warren was told all bets were off as we had to secure alternate investment due to his failure to complete on the deal. However, we decided to keep going with the application for Warren's Irish AOC as we had undertaken to do this as part of our original bargain. We didn't wish to be found in default of any of our obligations under the agreement we had entered into. We never actually got to finalise the AOC application as Warren, realising the difficulties and time lag for this course of action, gave up on the notion of having his own AOC and took off on another tack of utilising a UK-based licensed operator to provide the operations framework for his Italian BA franchise which, in all fairness to him, he did manage to get in the air later that year, with substantial backing from Italian investors.

We needed to pay a US$100,000 deposit that week to Titan to secure the aircraft, and another US$100,000 was required by Malmo Aviation as a goodwill down-payment on our intentions to purchase their leased aircraft later in the year. As Janesville would be involved as the lessor of one or both of these aircraft ultimately, we asked them to lend us the deposits. They agreed.

The due diligence went well and Chris Foyle signalled his intent to invest. But what I didn't know was that he didn't have that sort of cash readily available. He sent Neil Hansford, together with Peter Sorby, CEO of Air Foyle, to set up camp in Cityjet. The feeling of *déjà vu* was overpowering. *What is it about this business?* I asked myself many times. *Could this be happening again?* To be fair to Hansford in particular and Sorby, they were not trying to interfere but were lending their support while trying to gain a deeper understanding of our operation. Foyle was attempting to raise cash in the City in support of his proposed investment. We didn't have time for this as we were under pressure with the French, who understandably were looking for confirmation that we were solid. I had to short-circuit the process. I asked Peter Sorby to level with me about the money; what would it take to get Air Foyle the support it needed to make the investment? I speculated about Air France coming in for twenty-five per cent of the equity. Yes, that would do it, Sorby was certain. "OK, let's go to Paris and ask the man," I suggested.

There is only one way to ask someone like Bruno Matheu of Air France about something like this, and that's straight up. I led the conversation, tracing back over the Warren/Speedwing story and how all connections with British Airways-related interests had now been severed. Now we had a chance of support from Air Foyle, who were prepared to invest for a substantial controlling interest in Cityjet if Air France were willing to come in for twenty-five per cent. Bruno knew time was running out for Air France, as well as for us, to have everything in place for the summer season, which was practically on top of us. He also knew Cityjet potentially held the key to developing low-cost feed into the growing CDG hub. We were non-French, non-unionised and with a strong work ethic. I had been building this relationship over time and now it was time to test how strong it really was. He said "yes". Just like that. There would be conditions. There would be due diligence. It would have to be done before the summer programme started at the end of March. But that one little word of "yes" was so sweet.

Now the pressure on Chris Foyle to perform was enormous. He could not fail to produce the money on this, and he knew it. He would deliver the funds. He never told me from where, although I subsequently came to believe I knew the source. He was taking a big risk and I admire his guts for doing it.

The days were full of hours, each containing an unfolding component of a story that was weaving itself at a frantic pace. Butler hadn't finished with us. Having been rumbled at the Shelbourne Hotel, his father called in to bail him out and, with lawyers and accountants pursuing him in Dublin over unpaid bills, he wanted revenge. Of course, he also most probably lost out on stiffing Warren and others for aircraft deposits. He befriended a local air taxi operator in Dublin, who in turn put him in touch with a journalist in *The Irish Times*. A story ran which revealed details of the failed deal between Warren Seymour and Cityjet. Much was made of "documents" in the possession of *The Irish Times* which purported to support the theory that the Australians and the board of Cityjet were colluding to breach the EU regulations governing ownership of EU-registered airlines by non-EU citizens. The damage was done. I got a call from the Department of Public Enterprise demanding a full explanation. British Airways were looking for assurances from Warren that the Irish AOC application was not compromised by this revelation in the media. And there was more to come.

It was a Friday evening and I was having a meal with Neil Hansford at the airport hotel in Dublin. Paul White, our PR consultant, called me on my mobile. *The Irish Times* were running with a follow-up story tomorrow morning and this was a bad one. Again, the hand of Butler was obvious and this time he was really going for it. He was revealing details of our precarious financial position, all gleaned from the documents he had acquired from Warren or his associates, either by fair or foul means. This was a meltdown situation at ten o'clock on a Friday evening, with the deadline for printing coming up within the hour. "We've got to get the story pulled, Paul, or we're out of business," I screamed into my phone. "Are you nuts?" — or words very close to that, but perhaps less civil — came back at me in double-quick time. "What are you asking me to do?" Paul questioned me. "You've got to get to the editor tonight. This stuff is coming from a known crook. We can back this up; we can show him the file."

Paul went to the business editor's house at eleven o'clock and put his own reputation on the line for his client. He pleaded our case and Cliff Taylor, to his credit, pulled the story, but he left Paul in no doubt that our evidence better stack up. I met a very

agitated business editor the following Monday morning. I pushed
the file across the table to him. It took all of a couple of minutes
for Cliff Taylor to say he was delighted he had acted in stopping
the story. He personally and professionally had no time for ven-
detta-inspired planting of stories in his newspaper.

The French sent in their team to do the due diligence. It wasn't
the ideal way to spend St Patrick's Day. It was excruciatingly
tough, particularly as they were equally intent on doing a due
diligence on the forward business plan as well as examining what
had gone on in the past. Their appetite for financial modelling
was inexhaustible. One of the most difficult things to get them to
believe was exactly what had happened on the Warren Seymour
failed investment attempt. They could not grasp the notion that
the £1.75 million paid in was left so vulnerable to forfeit.

Then there was the row with the existing Irish shareholders.
Paul Coulson wanted some residual value to attach to the shareholding of the Irish investors. Bruno Matheu of Air France wasn't
having any of it. He took the hard line that the owners of the
company had allowed the airline get into this perilous state of financial tightness and they didn't deserve to be rewarded by being
allowed retain even a minimum equity stake. It was beginning to
get personal and nasty. These senior guys from Air France were in
their second or third long day in our offices and the strain was
beginning to tell. It was 19 March and after several attempts to
produce a simple but extremely comprehensive one-page "Heads
of Agreement", tempers were lost too often. This was a three-way
deal between Air Foyle, Air France and the existing Irish shareholders in Cityjet. The lack of sympathy for the Irish seemed to be
rooted in the view which the French took of Janesville being
owned by the shareholders in the airline, who were benefiting
from lease rentals from Cityjet. We made strenuous efforts to explain that, without the Janesville set-up and the clever aircraft financing deals which had been put in place over the past few
years, there would be no Cityjet. But the French didn't want to

know. Maybe it was a negotiating posture or maybe they just couldn't really imagine how hard-pressed Cityjet had been to survive this long.

It was 5.50 in the evening and Bruno especially wanted to catch the 6.15 plane to Paris. He was about to sign the final version of the summary Heads of Agreement when Paul Coulson raised one more point of clarification. Bruno misheard him and interpreted something entirely different. He flung the pen down and stormed out the door. I looked at Paul and I looked at the door still swinging behind a rapidly moving, irate Frenchman. I bolted after him. I got him at the elevator and I put my foot in the door. "You didn't hear him right, Bruno, come back inside and sign it off, please." He stared at me and without a word he charged back into the office, signed the paper, scowled at everyone and left again in a puff of high anxiety.

We had just got through another important gate. Of course, there would be a lot of forests cut down to produce the voluminous paper in the contracts giving force to what was written on that one page. The lawyers would earn their money and I would kill a good few more brain cells before I would see the money in the airline's account. But this was progress and having the French in as shareholders, as far as I was concerned, dramatically improved the prospects of Cityjet's long-term viability.

We got the Titan aircraft purchase deal completed with the help of Anglo Irish and Janesville and no thanks to Gene Wilson, the CEO of Titan Airways, who remained inflexible right up to the deadline he imposed on our closing on the contract. In fact, we were worried right up to signing the final papers that we could end up with no aircraft and lose our deposit.

Meanwhile, back to the big game; we hired the lawyers and I had no hesitation in recommending that Siobhan Lohan of A&L Goodbody should act for Air France, as this was a deal that had to be effected under Irish law. Air Foyle appointed their own choice of Irish law firms and after weeks of drafting documents, we were all off to Paris to attempt to close the deal on a given day. Even right up to the last minute there were disagreements between the lawyers on specific clauses. It was a struggle to keep everybody focused on the spirit of what we are all trying to achieve. We finally got to the point of signing by about 6.00 that evening and then we were invited to meet the Chairman of Air France and mark the occasion with a champagne toast. We dashed to terminal 2 and just made our last flight to Dublin.

The feeling of satisfaction on that flight home was immense because we had managed to pull a desperate situation back from the brink and get the airline re-capitalised with what we hoped would prove to be responsible investors. I was extremely proud of what had been achieved, particularly as I had had to do so much of the hard graft. Most of my co-directors had been blinded by the prospect of Warren Seymour and his experience as a successful airline operator. I empathised with their wanting a solution to the twin needs of a substantial investor and airline partner all in one. However, I was disappointed at their reluctance to back my judgement much earlier. In reality, they had missed the point that our management team had become, through sheer necessity, quite experienced at the business of running an airline and the constant quest for "an airline partner as investor" had become a bit of a hollow mantra.

Also, in spite of the very serious distractions and unwelcome interference over the previous three months, we still managed to get ourselves into position to start the additional new routes for Air France. We also migrated to their distribution system for all our routes and made the requisite changes in our infrastructure to facilitate the transition to the status of an Air France partner.

I had an ear-to-ear smile on that flight home and I had no shortage of buddies to murder a couple of pints with when we got on the ground.

Chapter Twenty-one

FIVE LOAVES, TWO FISHES AND TOO MANY COOKS

While we had managed to put enough resources in place for the commencement of the new Air France programme, when we looked at covering our own Cityjet routes it was a case of "five loaves and two fishes". We had five 146 series 200 aircraft, one 146 series 100 and two Saab 2000s. The 146s were tasked on Dublin/Paris, Paris/Florence, Paris/London City and Dublin/London City. We had one Saab on Strasbourg/London City and the remaining Saab on Toulouse/Madrid. We had no aircraft to operate Dublin/East Midlands and our weekend schedule on Dublin/Malaga. The Air France requirements at this stage were determining our fleet composition. Notwithstanding their earlier indications that they might have a requirement for us to operate up to five Saab 2000s, they leaned heavily back towards more BAe 146 capacity. Also, our confidence in Saab being able to support us with an expanded fleet of their aircraft was beginning to wane. We had terminated our arrangement with Regional Airlines where we were operating one of their Saab 2000s on our licence, on the Strasbourg/London City route. We gave them back the aircraft and re-converted the pilots back to 146 duty. But Air France contracted us directly with one of our remaining two Saabs to operate the Strasbourg service.

We had got the Dublin/East Midlands route very close to breakeven and we didn't think it made sense to abandon it at that point. So Neil Hansford, who was still constantly present with us on behalf of Air Foyle, came up with the idea of a wet lease of a BAe ATP sixty-eight-seat turboprop from British World Airways — their aircraft, their crew, operating under our flight numbers. The additional number of seats compared to the Saab gave us a sporting chance of cancelling out the penal charges of hiring in someone else's aircraft and billeting their crew in a hotel in Dublin all week throughout the summer season. The plan looked OK on paper. Just.

Dublin/Malaga was a bit different. We could not find another 146 anywhere. The Air Foyle people were confident of being able to sweat their network of contacts to procure one and things were looking promising in Australia where Ansett had decided to mothball a batch of low-time 146s. Neil Hansford was interacting with a personal contact of his in Ansett on the purchase of a particular aircraft and brought discussions to the point where we dispatched our engineering quality assurance manager to Australia for a detailed inspection of plane and records. The finance for this deal was potentially to come from another source dug up by Hansford in the US. In the almost seven-year history of Cityjet to this point, this was the first time I or any of the Cityjet management team had not been involved directly in orchestrating a deal on an aircraft. In many ways I was relieved and I took the view that there was other expertise now available to us from people longer on experience in this aviation business than me, so let them at it.

Even as I write this, I know that it sounds pathetically like an ego-fuelled defence of the airline's dependency on me. But the reality of those seven years was that a few of my colleagues and myself, through sheer necessity in responding to successive desperate episodes in a survival story, had actually built up an expertise in aircraft acquisition that was in many ways quite uniquely effective. Unfortunately, on this occasion, our confidence in the

Air Foyle team's expertise in aircraft acquisition was misplaced. While we waited for the Australian 146, we entered into a short-term wet lease, also from British World, of a BAC One-Eleven for our weekend scheduled services to Malaga. This was an expensive option given the fuel-guzzling characteristics of the One-Eleven, on top of the cost of accommodation of British crews in Dublin. The weeks slipped into months and there was still no sign of a conclusion of the deal to acquire the Australian 146. The bills kept coming in and we were now in a classic situation on both Dublin/East Midlands and Dublin/Malaga, seeing British World enjoy a guaranteed profit for their troubles while we racked up awful losses resulting from the enormous cost of paying another operator to fly for us on these two routes.

We were stretched and losing blood. The Air France programme had eaten up practically all of our operational resources but the revenue and the certainty of it made sense. To persist with East Midlands and Malaga without enough aircraft of our own was a mistake. Had the elusive additional 146 materialised, we would have avoided a bath on Malaga and given ourselves much needed strength in depth which would have saved us a fortune during the Saab fiasco, which was about to bite us very hard that summer. Then sticking with East Midlands to get it over the gain line might have been justified. But the additional 146 didn't happen. The efforts of the Air Foyle team working on this procurement came to nothing.

To really compound the situation where any possibility of achieving an operating margin was exported to third-party suppliers of wet-lease capacity, Saab had their finest hour.

An engine on one of our Saabs failed to start on an outbound flight from London City to Strasbourg. A Cityjet engineer was dispatched from Dublin on our next flight to the City with a new starter motor and his toolbox. He duly fitted the new starter and requested the crew to do a full-power engine run-up on the ground. The aircraft taxied out to the holding point at the end of the runway, without passengers of course, to firewall the throttles and check the engine performance readings. There was a mighty bang and part of the cowling was blown off. The Captain shut down the offending engine and returned to the stand. Together with the engineer, the crew observed that the trauma of this event had occasioned the engine to shift in its bolted position to the nacelle (a receptacle on the wing into which the engine is fitted) attached to the wing.

We called Saab. Nothing they could do for us. This was a new one to me. Saab held the aircraft type manufacturer licence for the 2000, yet they were attempting to pass us off to the vendor who actually made the nacelle assembly. This was a tiny French company who no one in our engineering department had ever heard of previously. When we eventually tracked them down, some days later — they had been on holiday with no help-desk facility in operation — they told us there was nothing they could do and suggested we get in touch with Westland. Westland apparently held the designs for this attachment of the nacelle to wing and engine. Not overly enthusiastic about helping to solve the problem, Westland took a degree of persuading to get them to come and visit the aircraft at London City. By now, the aircraft had been on the ground at City for five days and the work on even starting to design a solution had not begun. When the diagnosis was finally delivered, it was a thousand times worse than any of us could have imagined. There was literally no off-the-shelf fix. Quite simply, the manufacturer had not envisaged a problem of this nature, so there were no spare parts.

What we were now looking at was a major design which would have to undergo a manufacturer's approval process followed by the build of the bits by Westland and finally the attachment of the new assembly to the wing and the re-bolting on of a replacement engine. To add to our woes was Westland's objection to accomplishing the repairs "in the open" at London City as there was no hangar there and absolutely no possibility of flying the injured aircraft out of there on one engine to a customised heavy-maintenance facility. We overcame Westland's objections by constructing a temporary tent-like structure around and over the aircraft at LCY so that prolonged work could be carried out regardless of weather. The process creaked and groaned and by the time our aircraft was fit to fly out of London City, a full seven weeks had passed. The cost of hiring in aircraft to cover our commitments to Air France, combined with the cost of this expensive repair, came to £1 million. Despite our committed efforts over the preceding months, Saab did not cough up any meaningful contribution to our outlay or provide any credible explanation as to why the explosion occurred in the first place. I quickly came to the view that Saab's behaviour made BAe and the successive badges declaring ownership of the infamous ALF 502 engine on the 146 look comparatively very good, even on their bad days.

The stress began to show in Chris Foyle and his team, as the management accounts bore witness to the rapid diminution of the cash put in by Air France and himself. His senior people from Air Foyle were understandably challenged by the significant differences between a scheduled airline operation and that of a contract services provider, with which they were much more familiar. Up to then, Air Foyle never had to engage in the day-to-day commercial operation of an airline. Air Foyle's role in life had been to supply crew and flight operations management on contract to client airlines who took care of everything else. They decided to recruit a Chief Operations Officer to work closely with me. Their shortlist was whittled down to two candidates, whom Air France and I were asked to interview separately to give our views.

Jacques Bankir had taken early retirement from Air France a few short years previously after a distinguished career. He was no stranger to the personalities in Air France who had made the decision to get involved with Cityjet. The French connection apart, Jacques was an outstanding solution and his selection was unanimous. Being a consummate professional, Jacques's loyalty was always going to be to Cityjet, the company he was now charged with turning around. He was a rare talent with a reservoir of experience that I could scarcely believe. *Where has this guy been all of the past seven years of my purgatory?* was a question that ran through my mind. If only I could have had access to someone like Jacques much, much earlier, then maybe this story might have been different. But he was here now and we struck up an instant partnership.

There were tensions. Two owners: Air Foyle with £4 million sunk in the airline and Air France with a convertible loan of £2 million paid in. Air France had a vested interest in Cityjet staying alive, given the extent of the flying operation we were undertaking for them, and the revenue that it produced was crucial to the sustenance of our business. The airline was haemorrhaging as a result of the failure to obtain another two 146s to add to the fleet which had resulted in the extended hiring-in of third-party operated aircraft to continue the East Midlands and Malaga routes. It was all too obvious that for Cityjet's survival, a cash call was looming for the shareholders. For Chris Foyle to preserve his significant majority stake was going to take a substantial further commitment of capital. Air France would probably follow proportionately but the depth of their pockets was comparatively huge. Like a stricken air balloon, it was time to start thinking of jettisoning surplus weight. It was decided to stop the effort on Dublin/ East Midlands at the earliest contract break opportunity with British World on the wet lease of the BAe ATP. We knew we had to let Malaga run to the end of the summer season in October, as we had no way of accommodating the heavily booked loads with alternative carriers. So by powers of deduction, the very core of Cityjet's being, the Dublin/London City route was rounded on. The new shareholders deemed this route to be no longer core to the operation and if it could be sold off then that is what should be done.

While I was away for a short week's break in Malaga, the Air Foyle management met with Aer Lingus to open up discussions on the Dublin/London City route. On my return, when I learned that things had been moved forward quickly in my absence, I made my anger felt in very clear terms with Chris Foyle. Aer Lingus were not prepared to buy the route from us but they said they were interested in taking it over and doing a form of "damp" lease whereby Cityjet would operate on their behalf, providing aircraft and pilots, but Aer Lingus cabin crew would replace Cityjet's. The reason for my annoyance was twofold. Firstly, the fact that this had been initiated behind my back spoke volumes to me, especially as I had been nothing but totally up-front with the Air Foyle people from the start. The further irritation was that my hard-earned insight into the workings of the Aer Lingus corporate deal-making mindset was being bypassed.

Of course, the last thing I wanted to see was our efforts over the past years in carving out a niche route on Dublin/London City being handed on a plate to Aer Lingus who, in my certain view, had been waiting gleefully to dance on our grave. However, trying very hard to put personal prejudices to one side, I argued strenuously for at least the payment of a lump sum to transfer ownership of the route. There was also a huge issue around the Transfer of Undertaking Legislation (TUPE); what Aer Lingus were proposing was a blatant transfer of our cabin crew jobs. They also wanted Cityjet to indemnify Aer Lingus for any future claims that might be brought by Cityjet staff as a direct result of the route transfer. I decided to install myself into the negotiations on the basis that no involvement meant no control of the outcome. Behind the scenes I worked frantically to find an alternative deal. I had accepted the inevitability of letting go ownership of the route, but to see Aer Lingus smirk at what would be a "victory" in their terms? I was determined I was not going to allow that happen.

I had been developing a good relationship with Jersey European over the previous few months and we had much in common in that they operated a large fleet of 146s in addition to other types. But Jersey were also in a partnership relationship with Air France, operating a number of franchise routes including Birmingham to Paris and Heathrow to Toulouse and other south of France destinations. I worked hard on Jim French, joint CEO of Jersey European, to convince him of the merits of adding the Dublin route to his growing activity on other routes out of London City. So while I kept the subterfuge of trying to reach a deal with Aer Lingus going, I was in fact putting the final details to bed on a better arrangement with Jersey European.

Jersey agreed to pay us £0.5 million as a consideration for transferring the route to them, and they would also contract us to provide aircraft, pilots and cabin crew to operate on their behalf. Furthermore, we would still fly in Cityjet colours on the route for at least the first year and the whole deal would be presented to the market as a code share arrangement between the two airlines. All revenue would be given to Jersey, together with all operating costs, while Cityjet would receive a fixed price per flight. We signed, received the much needed cash . . . and, boy, were Aer Lingus pissed off.

Their riposte didn't take long. Within weeks, they announced they were going on the route in a head-to-head against us. They were granted slots by London City Airport with only five minutes' separation from our timings in our long-standing schedule. Aer Lingus were the dominant carrier on the overall route of Dublin to London, when their combined capacity on Heathrow, Stansted and Gatwick were aggregated against Ryanair to Stansted and Luton and ourselves to City. Given that City Airport had a finite market appeal, to put two flights in the system barely five minutes apart was essentially to divide the available traffic for that time of day among the competing carriers. The consequence of that would be that both airlines would operate at a loss. Furthermore, because Aer Lingus lacked sufficient 146 capacity they had wet-leased in a 146 from Flightline to operate on their behalf. This meant a dramatic increase in their costs of flying the route, which we estimated to be in the region of an additional £2 million over a year. All of this was tantamount to price-cutting from a dominant position to drive the smaller carrier off the route. This, in our opinion and that of our lawyers, was in clear breach of European Competition law.

I went to the Irish Competition Authority, who were hopelessly unequipped and less than interested in dealing with the issue in a speedy manner. Of course, Aer Lingus knew that no form of a policing action could be taken quickly against their predatory tactics and as their trouser pockets were deeper than Jersey European's and Cityjet's, it would only be a matter of time before we would have to toss the towel into the ring. I mounted a campaign in the media and the coverage was extensive and empathetic to our state of being under siege. I even had a meeting with the Tánaiste (Deputy Prime Minister), whose ministerial responsibility was Enterprise and Employment. She candidly admitted that the Competition Authority was ineffective and, while she proclaimed her empathy with the position we found ourselves in, there was frankly nothing she or the Government could to do in the near term. To her credit, she was honest and didn't hold out any false dawns. She told it as it was. Too bad if it meant competition law couldn't be upheld due to the failure of the Government to put the right machinery and resources in place.

Jersey stuck with the awful performance for a few more months and finally pulled the plug in March 2000. Aer Lingus then reduced their flight schedule from six returns per business day back to four and sat on the route, absorbing an operating loss to protect their high yield traffic on Heathrow. My earlier prophecy to London City management came to pass as they witnessed a reduction in passengers from 210,000 a year, which we provided them with, down to 160,000. No other carrier would go in now against Aer Lingus, because all knew the Irish national carrier would just turn up the heat with an increased frequency of flights until they burned off whoever dared to take them on.

The relationship between Air France and Air Foyle did not develop as it probably should have. I don't know if it was a French/English thing or just down to the particular personalities involved, but the chemistry certainly wasn't gelling. The growing pressures in the business from the cash drain of the non-Air France-related activities of Cityjet were now approaching melt-down point. The series of corrective measures that were being taken, including the canning of East Midlands and the sale of the Dublin/London City route, all pointed to improved figures going forward. However, the hole caused by the loss of service of the Saab 2000 aircraft for the best part of two months and the hiring-in to cover Malaga over a protracted period in the absence of the additional 146, which never happened, had all conspired to put a massive dent in the coffers. There was going to have be a cash call on the shareholders and Chris Foyle was not relishing the pros-pect of having to follow his initial investment. As that autumn of 1999 enveloped us, the intensity of the increasingly frequent meet-ings of the Board was gripping. Aidan Keane and myself were spending a lot of time on the production of forecasts based on emerging assumptions, which were dependant on the extent of the future flying activity Air France may or may not gift to Cityjet. What was emerging at these successive meetings, which were al-ways held in Paris, was a game of "chicken"; Air France were holding out on further financial support for Cityjet ahead of Air Foyle making a commitment to inject more investment capital into the airline.

When it became abundantly clear that Air Foyle was not dis-posed to make further investment in Cityjet, Air France took the initiative of opening talks with Jersey European with a view to persuading them to buy the Air Foyle majority stake in Cityjet. Throughout this protracted period of three months or so, Cityjet was perilously close to going bust yet again. Aidan Keane and Hugh Rodgers performed many miracles with scant cash re-sources to keep the company alive. For a while, it looked as if Jer-sey just might do a deal but, at the eleventh hour, they chose to link a takeover of Cityjet to securing concessions out of Air France on the franchise agreements they had in place over several routes.

This seemed to incense the French to the extent that a clear definition of the meaning of the word "non" was delivered in unambiguous terms.

With the inevitability of Cityjet's impending closure unless fresh capital was found, Air France made an approach to Air Foyle to acquire their majority stake in Cityjet for a lesser sum than that invested some nine months earlier. The deal was wrapped up pre-Christmas, with the formalities to be concluded in January. This would see Air Foyle depart as shareholders and Air France become the one hundred per cent owner of Cityjet. Substantial loans would be advanced by Air France to Cityjet to stabilise the airline and growth plans would be drawn up.

And so, not for the first time had a significant shareholder in Cityjet come and gone in less than a year. Such was the pace of life in this small regional airline that refused to die.

I had sympathy for Chris Foyle, because he had bravely stepped forward with cash only a few months earlier. I think it went wrong for him because he relied too heavily on some of those around him, who simply were unable to navigate their way through the very demanding business environment of a scheduled airline in a highly competitive arena. The Air Foyle business to that point had been highly risk-averse. They would provide their customers with a licensed framework which included crew and technical support, but the customer took all of the risk around aircraft financing, operating costs and the marketing of bums on seats. The best decision Chris made was appointing Jacques Bankir as COO of Cityjet. However, a number of Air Foyle managers continued to "parachute in" on us, which fostered the rapid development of a "two camps" atmosphere. Things got bad when Chris appointed his new Managing Director of Air Foyle. He chose the unsuccessful candidate for the Cityjet COO position, which was in my view a big mistake. This man attempted to impose himself on the Cityjet management and his aggressive style created a mood of hostility. Alienating the hard-pressed manage-

ment team who were doing a pretty good job in tough circumstances was not clever and in many ways frustrated the course of
remedial action on a far-too-frequent basis. The Cityjet gig was a
million miles different from anything anyone in Air Foyle had
done before and, sadly, Chris paid a very high price for the experience.

Chapter Twenty-two

NO MEDALS, BUT WE KNOW WHAT WE ACHIEVED

Our seventh Christmas as an operating airline came and City-jet was still in business and looking pretty certain to stay in business well into the future as a soon-to-be wholly owned subsidiary of Air France.

The airline was now parked in a very safe harbour and the jobs of a very loyal and committed staff were no longer in doubt. Jacques Bankir was a forceful manager who could apply his considerable experience in this tough business and leverage his unrivalled insight into the workings of Air France to optimise the opportunities for Cityjet. With an expanding fleet in prospect of a surge in more flying activity with the French, our engineering department was gearing up under the capable direction of Mick Maher, who we had prised out of Aer Lingus some months earlier. Our Flight Operations department was swiftly moving out of fire-fighting mode, where through circumstance it had been for far too long, into a more organised unit with the time and resources to plan ahead in order to minimise surprises. Geoff White, who I had brought in on a three-month consultancy to reorganise our crew resource management, had now been with us for a year and had brought huge stability to this vital area. Geoff would eventually not only stay with Cityjet but would ultimately assume the role of CEO after Jacques Bankir's return to France some two years later.

The French were adamant that Cityjet would remain an Irish-registered company and an Irish-licensed airline. This was important especially as Cityjet was non-unionised. Staff worked in accordance with the regulations laid down by the Irish Aviation Authority and the Department of Enterprise and Employment and not in accord with "negotiated" terms and conditions heavily influenced by trade unions. The cost of employing staff on an Irish payroll is considerably lower than most countries in Europe, where the "social" cost of employment can be penal. But more than any of this was the simple and well-proven fact that the staff in Cityjet were willing, flexible and hugely committed to giving 110 per cent in terms of effort. This was the Cityjet culture that we had nurtured through incredibly difficult years and it now had become the norm for the way people wanted their work to be.

My emotions were running high as we entered the new millennium. I knew that my job was done and it was time to move on. This feeling was no stranger to me, as we had met before. Ten years previously, I had the same lump to swallow when I realised that leaving my beloved Savings and Investments, where I had played a pivotal role in building up the company over seventeen years, was the inevitable next step. It is very, very hard to take yourself out of the middle of something that has had such a big part of you over a sustained period of time. My style of leadership has always been one of total immersion in the business and not asking people to do things I'm not prepared to do myself. I had absolutely lived and breathed the Cityjet business every day of the previous seven-and-a-half years. There was never a moment in that time when I was bored or wondering what to tackle next. I might not have known exactly how I was going to try to resolve issues but squaring up to them was never in doubt. The impact I had on the life of Cityjet and the impact it had on me was huge. This separation was going to bring enormous relief, probably for both the company and myself, but the pain would be all for me to feel. Walking away is not easy. Stepping off a very fast rotating wheel and attempting to stand up straight without feeling dizzy is some trick.

But moving on was what I knew I needed to do. Air France is an enormous organisation and they run things in a highly efficient manner. They are a very structured company with tremendous discipline in planning and reporting, and decision-making has a protracted timeframe and a rigid protocol to be observed. *I'm an entrepreneur*, I told myself. This was not an environment where my particular style of making things happen "in the now" would thrive. The new Cityjet would require a different form of leadership with compliance with the new shareholder's wishes and no decision-making "on the fly". There would be politics to be played and, I felt, *that's not my kind of gig.*

So, as January drew to a close, I called the staff together in the large open space in our Atrium office at the top of the terminal building and gave them the news. I felt strangely similar to how I had felt that time, some years earlier, when I had to address the staff and tell them we were going into examinership. Then, I was hoping they would have confidence in me when I told them their jobs would be safe and that we would get out the other end with a recapitalised airline. Now, I felt as if I was deserting them and I hoped they would understand that there really was no other possible outcome. The journey through all of the turbulence was over. The fire-fighting was a thing of the past. There would be space granted by suppliers and better terms in virtually every deal based on the strength of the name of the new shareholder. There was no more need to fight for recognition of the Cityjet brand in a crowded market place. The brand now was Air France, by Cityjet. The enormous marketing and distribution machine, with truly global reach, which Air France possessed would take care of grabbing market share.

I would not be the only one leaving; sadly, the writing was on the wall for our in-house sales, marketing, reservations, public relations and commercial functions. The Air France global distribution power was going to take over those functions as everything we would do from now on would be branded as Air France flights.

Given the emerging disproportionate level of flight activity at Dublin compared to Paris, it was also economically inevitable that the airline should now get out of the business of ground services such as check-in, ticket sales desk, flight dispatch and push-back. Jacques Bankir had initiated talks with Group Crit, a French manpower company with an extensive ground-handling operations business at Paris CDG. A deal was done which would see the French company purchase the ground-handling division of Cityjet to form the base of their entry into the third-party handling business in Dublin. The net effect of these happenings would be a reduction in staff numbers of close on 100, leaving a very lean 300-strong force on which to build expansion, focused on a core of flying more routes for Air France.

Accepting that these changes were economically essential, we had in Jacques Bankir a fantastic man who I was absolutely certain would keep the wellbeing of Cityjet and its staff uppermost in his mind as he would cleverly position Cityjet to optimise the growth opportunities within the Air France framework. That most definitely took the sting out of it for me because I knew I was handing over to a CEO who was far more competent than I could ever have been in leading the team in pursuit of success going forward in this new environment. I also had seen how Jacques had become smitten with the Cityjet spirit to survive and win and it was very obvious that he was genuinely enjoying his honorary Dubliner status.

I had six weeks to go to my departure from my position as CEO. I would remain connected to Cityjet, as the French had invited me to take on the role of non-executive chairman. I used the time to get my head set for a massive reduction in pace of life. Of course, there would be some form of leaving ceremony organised by the company but, quite separate to any such event, I was determined to go out in style. So Jane and I planned to throw our own party at the original scene of the crime: the Wanderers pavilion in Lansdowne Road, where we had held the very first Cityjet bash back in 1993. I had a very special guest list covering those people who had contributed their respective special bit in this story. This included past and present staff members and also people outside of the airline who were very closely involved. The support from some of them to the company and from others to me personally had been immeasurable. We had a night. I was high on emotion in making my final speech in a Cityjet context. It was perhaps the most difficult speech I have had to make, especially as that hand-picked audience knew so much about what really had gone on behind the scenes and just how tough and yet so exhilarating life had been for us over the past number of years.

And that was it. I had come through the most incredible business experience of my life where, against impossible odds, we had endured. But, in so many ways, this was not a business story. This really was a tale of a small bunch of people who could be accused of being naïve to attempt the thing in the first place. It was about digging deeper than any of us imagined we could go to find the resolve and the successive stream of initiatives to overcome the obstacles. It was about an infectious will to not let the airline die, no matter what. It was about not being paralysed by the constant fear of failure but determining to succeed.

There were no medals given out for distinguished service or bravery above and beyond the call of duty. There was no public recognition of what had been achieved by the people in Cityjet. The headlines all belonged to Ryanair, whose gravity-defying feats continued to send their share price soaring. Low-cost, no-frills airlines were what captured the imagination of the commentators. Success was defined in terms of the growth in monetary value of the business. As far as I was concerned, that was OK; that's the way the world works: *show me your money and I will tell you how much of a success you've been.*

But I had learned over the course of this journey that success is not necessarily about money. Yes, making money was of course our fundamental objective when we embarked on the plan to put the airline together. Investors were attracted to risk their own capital in a calculated gamble which held out the prospect of a handsome return. With each successive round of funding, the ambition was to protect the historic investment by providing the airline with enough oxygen to grow its way out of trouble. Remarkably, and quite contrary to what Cityjet watchers at the time would have understood, those investors who stayed the distance and participated in the inventive re-financing and leasing deals of four aircraft to Cityjet through the special-purpose leasing vehicle, Janesville, recovered money in excess of what they had cumulatively invested in the airline.

The three senior creditors who supported the examinership at the end of 1996 were compensated for their losses through expanded and uninterrupted trade with Cityjet, which is ongoing to this day.

Air France, the eventual owners of Cityjet after so many shareholders coming in and going out, are enjoying a very satisfactory return on their investment. Not only are they enjoying strong profit performance from their wholly owned subsidiary, but they also benefit enormously from the low-cost feed of passengers that Cityjet's fleet of sixteen jets, backed up by 550 dedicated staff, bring to the Air France network hub at Paris CDG.

I always had a deeply rooted belief that we would make Cityjet endure and get to a place where it could be successful in commercial terms. I am thrilled that those investors and creditors who kept faith with me and hung in there on a knife edge got their rewards ultimately. Air France deserve to reap success from what was a brave move for them against a difficult economic and industrial relations background at home.

In looking back, there were some things which, if we were starting now we could have taken advantage of. For a start, had the internet been around, we would not have been at the mercy of the travel agents who controlled the bookings of their corporate

clients. This meant us having to match the exorbitant rates of commission — as much as fifteen per cent — being offered by Aer
Lingus and British Midlands to freeze us out. With the internet,
corporate passengers can book directly themselves and there is no
commission to be paid out. The BAe 146 is a much more dependable aircraft to operate these days thanks to improvements made
by the engine manufacturers and the considerable knowledge
base built up by operators like Cityjet. This could have meant the
difference in operating a high-frequency dependable service to the
business community.

And what about the money I didn't make or, more to the
point, the money I gave up the opportunity to make by doing
something else over those fast years? Well, that still bothers me.
There were times I could have and probably should have got out,
taken the consequences of the airline failing, and moved on into a
smarter venture. I could have used my energy and initiative to
engage in an easier business. When I started, I had a reasonable
ambition to make a serious amount of capital out of the business
through establishing the airline, stabilising it and then selling it
on. With each successive round of fundraising and the never-
ending changing of the guard through so many different shareholders, I remained in all that time core to the operation going
forward. I continued to entertain the hope that I would ultimately
get rewarded if the airline could get over the gain line in terms of
turning a profit. But as the going became increasingly tough, I re-
prioritised my objectives. Making the thing survive and protecting the jobs of those whose colossal efforts were keeping Cityjet in
the air became my preoccupation.

Would I do it again? Knowing, of course, what I know now,
my answer would have to be "no", because the price was too
high. Not just in terms of money not made for myself but much
more so in terms of the cost to my family life and the risk I took
with my health. The latter point probably didn't strike me as I was
going through it, but when I look back at myself and the state I

had got into under the unrelenting pressure and sheer pace of trying to stay ahead of a rapidly unfolding saga, I realise I put myself
dangerously close to breakdown for far too long.

Any positives? Loads of them — and I know that probably
sounds contradictory. Saying I would not do it again does not
mean I regret doing it in the first place. In fact, being totally honest with myself, I have to say I would not have missed it for anything. It was the most extraordinary opportunity to be associated
with that I can imagine. It was probably the closest I could have
got to in peacetime to get even a tiny clue as to what it must have
been like for people committed to endure through major conflicts
like the Battle of Britain and the blitz of London. It was a phenomenal non-stop experience, facing huge challenges daily on top
of dealing with the routine tasks of running the business. It was
about teamwork. It was about digging so deep to find another
spark that might ignite a problem-solving initiative. It was about
constantly motivating people and in turn being motivated by
them to keep going. It was about building a business proposition
that was absolutely wrapped around serving our passengers'
needs. It was about committing to that proposition and letting it
dictate how and why we did everything from that point on.

It was about taking the development and management of relationships to heights I never knew were possible. Our currency
was trust built on complete honesty. In so many ways, we were
the Ronseal airline. Written on the outside of our tin was what
could be found on the inside. People knew where they stood with
us and what they could expect, whether they were a passenger, a
supplier or an investor.

We were successful. The people who were there and who
shared this journey with me know they were successful. We are all
richer, in the terms that really matter, for having done what we did.

EPILOGUE

I take immense pride in seeing Cityjet move forward strongly with its staff of more than 500, a fleet of sixteen jets and operating high-frequency routes out of Paris and Dublin to places like Florence, Zurich, Amsterdam, Gothenburg, Edinburgh, London and Malaga. I carry a wry smile these days with Cityjet back operating the Dublin/London City service, following the departure of Aer Lingus, who decided to rationalise their fleet in terms of the number of aircraft types they would fly. Cityjet has made money in each of the past three years, returning a profit of €7 million in its most recent year ending March 2004. Cityjet's current profitability is due to the enormous distribution power of Air France combined with the comparatively low cost of operations of Cityjet. The airline under my leadership was always under-capitalised and hugely dependant on our own distribution capability as well as the routes we were operating for Air France. It was the switch to total dependency on Air France marketing, the injection of sufficient capital by the French to bring the fleet size to critical mass and the coming to fruition of the efficiency in operations which we were progressively moving towards that has produced the success that is there now. The determination to keep going until a deal with the right partner, whom I was certain had to be Air France from as far back as 1996, has been proven beyond doubt to have been a commercially justifiable obsession.

Yes, we were naïve but most worthwhile things only get built because someone is naïve enough to try and is then totally committed to make it happen, no matter what. I could stand criticised as being the fool who only got the red nose while Air France are enjoying the whiskey. I genuinely say, the very best of luck to them. They recognised a good opportunity and put their money in. They took a chance and they deserve all of the commercial rewards that flow as a result. They had a huge respect for the people in Cityjet with their incredible commitment to getting the job done and serving the passenger first, always. They resisted the temptation of any acquiring company to impose their own management. They backed the Irish team and it has worked wonderfully well for everybody.

I also sometimes look back even a little further to Savings & Investments, which is now known as Cornmarket and majority owned by Irish Life and Permanent. It is going strong, with a staff of 200 making it probably the biggest brokers in Ireland.

It hasn't all been that bad. I was lucky to get the opportunity to play two halves of the game on two distinctly unique pitches. I have worked with great people over my career and I have good memories and learning from my journey of experience.

And what about me? What am I doing these days? Well, I set up an operation which I called Rainmaker Business Catalysts and, together with my partners Brendan Fuller and Gary Owens, we put our grey hairs to work to make serious business development happen for our customers. We're not consultants writing prescriptions to make companies better. Our focus is in converting strategy into real action. We bring pragmatic front-line experience and skills, not theory. And we have taken our own medicine. We are gainfully employed mainly in the financial services and public transport sectors.

Making it rain when and where it needs to; there's nothing quite like it.

INDEX